**Robert M** Center for th sor of law at teacher and Justice Will Court in 1962–63. After a decade of teaching law at the University of California-Berkeley, he entered administration as provost of the University of Cincinnati, followed by a term as vice-president of Indiana University at Bloomington, and five years as president of the University of Wisconsin System before becoming president of the University of Virginia in 1985. He has written many law review articles and several books, including *Classrooms in the Crossfire* (a study of textbook and curriculum censorship). He has chaired the National Association of State Universities and Land-Grant Colleges and the Commission on the Future of Virginia's Judicial System, and he has held high posts in the American Association of University Professors, the Carnegie Foundation for the Advancement of Teaching, the Educational Testing Service, the Commonwealth Fund, the Johnson Foundation, and the James River Corporation.

## Also in this series

THE RIGHTS OF ALIENS AND REFUGEES
THE RIGHTS OF AUTHORS, ARTISTS, AND OTHER
   CREATIVE PEOPLE
THE RIGHTS OF CRIME VICTIMS
THE RIGHTS OF EMPLOYEES AND UNION
   MEMBERS
THE RIGHTS OF INDIANS AND TRIBES
THE RIGHTS OF LESBIANS AND GAY MEN
THE RIGHTS OF OLDER PERSONS
THE RIGHTS OF PATIENTS
THE RIGHTS OF PRISONERS
THE RIGHTS OF RACIAL MINORITIES
THE RIGHTS OF SINGLE PEOPLE
THE RIGHTS OF STUDENTS
THE RIGHTS OF TEACHERS
THE RIGHTS OF WOMEN
THE RIGHTS OF YOUNG PEOPLE
THE RIGHT TO PROTEST
YOUR RIGHT TO GOVERNMENT INFORMATION
YOUR RIGHT TO PRIVACY

AN AMERICAN CIVIL LIBERTIES UNION HANDBOOK

# THE RIGHTS OF PUBLIC EMPLOYEES

## THE BASIC ACLU GUIDE TO THE RIGHTS OF PUBLIC EMPLOYEES

**SECOND EDITION**
Completely Revised and Updated

## Robert M. O'Neil

General Editor of the Handbook Series
Norman Dorsen, President, ACLU 1976–1991

SOUTHERN ILLINOIS UNIVERSITY PRESS
CARBONDALE AND EDWARDSVILLE

96   95   94   93      4   3   2   1

**Library of Congress Cataloging-in-Publication Data**

O'Neil, Robert M.
    The rights of public employees : the basic ACLU guide to the
rights of public employees / Robert M. O'Neil. — 2d ed.,
completely rev. and updated.
    p.   cm. — (An American Civil Liberties Union handbook)
    Rev. ed. of: The rights of government employees, 1978.
    1. United States—Officials and employees. 2. Employee rights—
United States. 3. Employee-management relations in government—
Law and legislation—United States. I. O'Neil, Robert M. Rights of
government employees. II. Title. III. Series.
KF5337.05    1993
342.73′068—dc20
[347.30268]                                                    93-17474
ISBN 0-8093-1927-6                                                 CIP
ISBN 0-8093-1928-4 (pbk.)

The paper used in this publication meets the minimum requirements of
American National Standard for Information Sciences—Permanence of
Paper for Printed Library Materials, ANSI Z39.48-1984. ∞

*To Karen*

# Contents

Preface     ix

Acknowledgments     xi

Introduction     xiii

I.   Public Employment and Individual Rights: An Overview     1

II.   The Threshold of Public Employment: Initial Qualifications     11

III.   Public Employment and Freedom of Speech     26

IV.   Politics, Patronage, Public Service, and Unions     49

V.   The Private Lives of Public Employees     73

VI.   Race, Gender, and Disability Discrimination     98

VII.   Procedural Rights of Public Employees     120

VIII.   The Legal System     142

# Preface

This guide sets forth your rights under present law and offers suggestions on how they can be protected. It is one of a continuing series of handbooks published in cooperation with the American Civil Liberties Union (ACLU).

Surrounding these publications is the hope that Americans, informed of their rights, will be encouraged to exercise them. Through their exercise, rights are given life. If they are rarely used, they may be forgotten and violations may become routine.

This guide offers no assurances that your rights will be respected. The laws may change, and in some of the subjects covered in these pages, they change quite rapidly. An effort has been made to note those parts of the law where movement is taking place, but it is not always possible to predict accurately when the law *will* change.

Even if laws remain the same, their interpretation by courts and administrative officials often varies. In a federal system such as ours there is a built-in problem since state and federal laws differ, not to speak of the variations among states. In addition, there is much diversity in the ways in which particular courts and administrative officials interpret the same law at any given moment.

If you encounter what you consider to be a specific abuse of your rights, you should seek legal assistance. There are a number of agencies that may help you, among them ACLU affiliate offices, but bear in mind that the ACLU is a limited-purpose organization. In many communities there are federally funded legal service offices that provide assistance to persons who cannot afford the costs of legal representation.

In general, the rights that the ACLU defends are freedom of inquiry and expression; due process of law; equal protection of the laws; and privacy. The authors in this series have discussed other rights (even though they sometimes fall outside the ACLU's usual concern) in order to provide as much guidance as possible.

These books have been planned as guides for the people directly affected: thus the question-and-answer format. (In some areas there are more detailed works available for experts.) These guides seek to raise the major issues and inform the nonspecialist of the basic law on the subject. The authors of these books are themselves specialists who understand the need for information at "street level."

If you encounter a specific legal problem in an area discussed in one of these handbooks, show the book to your attorney. Of course, he or she will not be able to rely exclusively on the handbook to provide you with adequate representation. But if your attorney hasn't had a great deal of experience in the specific area, the handbook can provide helpful suggestions on how to proceed.

> Norman Dorsen, General Editor
> Stokes Professor of Law
> New York University School of Law

# Acknowledgments

Any work reflects contributions far beyond those of the author. I have a special debt to several University of Virginia law students who have labored most effectively in various phases of this project—Stephen Smith (a 1992 graduate soon to clerk for Justice Thomas), Joan McKenna (a current student with substantial ACLU experience), and most especially Stephen Benz, a current student with unique understanding of the field, who made manifold contributions at a critical stage. Cameron Quinn, a former student from the 1980s, gave invaluable insight and guidance in regard to chapter IV.

Appreciation is also due to my Thomas Jefferson Center colleagues—Sarah Parker Johnson, Joan Hairfield, and Julie Lynn—who bore nobly and most supportively the diversions and distractions of this project. David Ratliff was invaluable in meeting unexpected challenges posed by new technologies. More was asked of each of these colleagues because of the pressures that deadlines and commitments inevitably impose. To each goes a special word of thanks.

# Introduction

This second and substantially revised edition marks more than simply a timely title change. The earlier focus on "government employees" has been replaced by the broader designation "public employees"—not only to reflect more accurately the scope of the work, but quite as much to stress the public service nature of the occupations and professions that constitute the subject. At a critical time in the evolution of the public workforce, such recognition seems appropriate.

Certain themes have remained relatively calm and constant during the nearly a decade and a half between first and second editions. There has, for example, been little activity in areas such as loyalty oaths and political or religious tests for public employment. Despite persistent efforts at repeal or modification, the curbs imposed by the Hatch Act on public employees' political activity remained unchanged throughout the 1980s and into the 1990s. The basic rights of public workers to speak out on matters of general importance had been well marked at the time of the first edition and have simply been refined in the intervening years. In these and other areas, the task of a second edition has mainly been to review and reaffirm.

Yet the areas that have seen major change far outweigh those that have been tranquil. Such dramatic developments as drug testing and AIDS testing, for example, profoundly reshape the analysis. The elimination of virtually all mandatory retirement effects another dramatic change. If patronage dismissal had been barred on constitutional grounds a decade ago, the legality of patronage hiring remained a serious question until 1900, when the Supreme Court extended the ban to all forms of party affiliation as a factor in public employment.

There have been major changes in the scope of physical privacy, apart from testing for drugs and disease. In the areas of race and gender discrimination, both Congress and the courts have been active in ways that call for major reexamination in a second edition. And the procedural rights of public employees have recently received major attention from both lawmakers and judges. In fact, a major reform of the federal civil service system, which has implications far beyond hearing rights, was already under way at the time of the first edition and took effect soon after its publication.

These and other changes in content will readily become apparent. In format, however, the new edition closely emulates its predecessor. The groupings of major topics and the question-and-answer format seem to have served well and are thus retained in familiar form in this new edition. Notes appear, as before, at the close of each chapter.

# THE RIGHTS OF
# PUBLIC EMPLOYEES

# Public Employment and Individual Rights: An Overview

People who work for the government live lives and have experiences that differ in important ways from their friends and neighbors who hold jobs in private business. Not only are they paid from public funds, they are assigned to perform tasks of public importance. Such persons have chosen to work for government rather than for a private firm, often for reasons that have little to do with the actual tasks they perform. Yet government employees are expected to shape and adapt their lives in ways not required of the rest of the workforce. This book begins by identifying and explaining some of those differences.

## May government deny a person a job on any ground or for any reason it chooses?

No. It is true that government does not "owe" any person a job, and no citizen has a constitutional right to a job. But a public agency that hires workers must consider every applicant on the basis of its needs and his or her qualifications. People cannot be turned away for reasons that are plainly arbitrary or discriminatory. Some grounds for denying employment are undeniably invalid. Race, gender, and religious preference (or lack of it) are obvious examples. And for most public jobs, political party affiliation may no longer be considered, though patronage once played a central role in government hiring.

Beyond these readily suspect criteria, the analysis is more difficult. Many other factors, apart from job skills and experience, may and do enter the equation. Not all such nonskill qualifications are invalid. Most of this book is devoted, in fact, to analyzing standards that may or may not be used to determine eligibility for public employment.

There was a time when government could hire and fire people pretty much at the whim or liking of the agency head. A century ago, the eminent Justice Oliver Wendell Holmes (then a Massachusetts state court judge) wrote that "a man may have a right to talk politics, but not to be a policeman"[1]—a maxim that led the court to uphold the firing of a Boston patrolman just for taking a role in partisan politics.

This view died hard. As late as 1952, the Supreme Court held that public school teachers who objected on grounds of conscience to swearing a loyalty oath were "at liberty to take their beliefs and associations and go elsewhere" if they did not "choose to work on such terms."[2]

Much has happened in the last half century to change this notion of public employment as a "privilege." Courts no longer reject the claims of government workers in so callous a fashion. As the result of decisions that began in the 1960s and continued through the ensuing decades, the rights of public employees have acquired a far firmer foundation.

The Supreme Court has often made clear that "public employment . . . may not be conditioned upon the surrender of constitutional rights which could not be abridged by direct government action."[3] This newer approach—often termed the doctrine of "unconstitutional conditions"—reflects a growing concern for the rights not only of people who work for the government but for all those who depend upon government for other benefits such as housing, welfare, and scholarships.[4]

This doctrine has special force in the area of employment. The courts have recognized that government dominates job opportunities in many fields; indeed, in some it has a virtual monopoly, so that a ban on *public* employment could effectively keep a person out of *all* employment. While teachers, security officers, nurses, bus drivers, and others may still find jobs in the private sector, the nonpublic options are few and dwindling.

The law has changed, and surely for the public employee's benefit. But before concluding that all is well, we must note one ominous cloud that recently appeared on the constitutional horizon. In the spring of 1991, the Supreme Court sustained the so-called gag rule that bars workers at federally funded health clinics from giving advice about abortion.[5] The case did not deal precisely with public employment. In fact, the majority opinion distinguished important public worker precedents. Yet the doctrine of unconstitutional conditions was seriously questioned and limited for the first time in three decades.

The abortion gag-rule case contained some hints that sound uncomfortably like the old "keep your views and work elsewhere" language of the 1950s—for example, in the suggestion that doctors who wished to give their patients abortion counseling remained free to do so on their own time at nonfederally supported clinics. It is not yet clear how far this decision erodes the protection that public workers have gained, though the Supreme Court's more grudging view of the rights of government beneficiaries bears close watching.

**Do public employees, as citizens, enjoy the same rights and liberties as people who work in the private sector?**

For the most part they do, but not completely. Gradual changes in the law have extended to public workers many of the rights and liberties of private citizens. But certain important differences remain. Courts have stopped short of conferring the full range of freedoms on public workers. Those who work for the federal government are, for example, barred from taking part in a wide range of partisan political activities in which their neighbors may freely engage.[6] Some communities demand that their employees live within the city limits.[7] Dress and grooming requirements have been imposed on certain public service positions and have been upheld by the courts.[8] Some groups of government workers may be required to undergo tests for drug use; their lockers and desks may be subject to search; or they may be asked to disclose certain financial data[9]—even though the personal privacy rights of nonpublic workers would protect against similar intrusions.

Of course many persons who work for private firms may be subject to similar rules. But the critical difference is that in their case it is the corporate employer and not the government that limits their freedoms and activities. And for that reason the public worker may actually have prospects of protection or relief not available to his or her private sector neighbor. For government's policies are always subject to the constraints of the Bill of Rights, even if they may eventually pass muster in court. Thus the person who objects to being asked to wear a dark business suit or dress on the job has little recourse when the edict comes from a private computer manufacturer, but when the employer is a government agency, the rule can at least be challenged in court.

**Do all public employees enjoy the same measure of rights and liberties?**

Clearly they do not. There are vast differences within the

public workforce. Military personnel, for example, have fewer rights than most other people who work for government.

Even among civilian jobs, there are important variations. Police officers are constrained in certain ways and to degrees that apply to few others. Some types of testing have been upheld only where the sensitive nature of the job or the agency mission clearly justified such intrusions. Certain qualities or attributes may be important in one job but not in others; a seriously overweight emergency technician or prison guard may pose risks that an overweight telephone operator or file clerk or, for that matter, agency head clearly would not. A former drug user might be tolerated as a custodian far more comfortably than would the same person as an air traffic controller.

The courts have come increasingly to recognize these differences. They tend to scrutinize more closely the relationship between the particular job and the specific rule rather than invoking broad or sweeping principles about what public employees may and may not be required to do. But not all courts are so sensitive. We will encounter situations in which rules and policies are still applied and sustained much more broadly than the logic or need would seem to warrant.

### Which laws define the rights of public employees?

Certain basic protections come from the Bill of Rights of the United States Constitution. Those safeguards now apply to the states as well—not only to state legislatures but also to administrative agencies, courts, and to all levels of local government. The constitutions of most states have similar provisions; in fact a state constitution may sometimes protect privacy or freedom of speech or worship more fully than the federal Bill of Rights, and when that is the case, the higher state standard prevails.

Much of the law that protects government workers now comes in statutory form. Laws like the Civil Rights acts of the 1960s, with the major 1991 amendments, the Age Discrimination in Employment Act, the Rehabilitation Act, and many others adopted by Congress during the last thirty years profoundly shape the climate within which government employees work. These laws often go beyond what the Constitution guarantees. Legislatures may add to, but may not take away, what the Constitution ensures. The basic guarantees of the Bill of Rights provide a floor but not a ceiling.

Administrative rules also define the rights and responsibilities of government workers, and may be extremely complex. Until the late summer of 1992, for example, there were no fewer than eighteen different versions of each and every regulation governing civilian personnel who worked for the Defense Department. The entire set of rules ran to some thirty thousand pages. Finding the precise version that applied presented a daunting task for civilian employees in the military. Now the Pentagon has combined and simplified the rules into a single version that applies to all civilian personnel.[10] But bewildering arrays of parallel rules still exist elsewhere in the public service.

Collective bargaining offers a good example of how wide are the variations in the laws that shape public employment. The Constitution ensures only that government workers may not be punished or fired because they belong to a union. Some state laws go much further in requiring government agencies to bargain with unions and even give workers the right to strike if negotiations fail. Other states flatly forbid public sector bargaining and make unlawful not only strikes but even negotiations with a union. In between these extremes is the model that essentially exists in the federal government; limited bargaining is permitted and controlled, but strikes are unlawful.[11]

Given such differences as these, it is obviously not possible to give categorical answers to questions like "May a public employee go on strike over wages and working conditions?" or "Must a government agency bargain with its workers or their union?" The only accurate answer is "that depends" or "it varies all over the map." Such variations exist in most areas where the Constitution does not provide a uniform national standard. They are simply a fact of life, and part of the complex pattern of public employment.

### Do employees of private business enjoy similar rights?

Not necessarily, though the differences are diminishing. In fact there are variations in both directions. Private workers have broader rights to engage in collective bargaining and to go on strike, for example, but may also enjoy fewer safeguards in such areas as privacy at the workplace, or the right to criticize publicly the employer's policies or practices.

In important ways, the two sets of interests are converging. Government funding or control or the exercise of a governmental function may subject some private employers to the full range of public responsibilities to their workers, on the theory that they are really performing a governmental role. And legislative action has steadily reduced these differences. In the summer of 1992, for example, extensive provisions of the Rehabilitation Act (which had applied only to public employers since its adoption in 1973) were broadened by Congress to cover nearly all private employers as well. Thus an important public-private disparity has now ended.

Meanwhile, the courts have begun to narrow the doctrine of "employment at will," which historically left a private employee subject to firing for just about any reason, or for no reason, in the absence of a contract or agreement. Courts in states like California have limited private employers' options in substantial ways and have found public policy grounds on which to order a discharged worker reinstated.[12] Thus a private employee who refuses to carry out what he or she believes is an unlawful order, or who "blows the whistle" on the employer may be protected by general principles of law even in the absence of statutory or contractual safeguards. The law in this area is evolving rapidly and differs dramatically from state to state. For further information about the private sector, see, in this series, *The Rights of Employees* (1993), by Wayne N. Outten, Robert J. Rabin, and Lisa R. Lipman.

### Do applicants for public employment have legal rights?

Yes, in many cases, and those rights are increasingly the same as the rights of people who already hold government jobs. Take politics as a case in point: In the 1960s the Supreme Court held that a public worker could not be fired for belonging to the "wrong" party or refusing to join the "right" party. For years thereafter, though, it was assumed that patronage hiring, as distinct from patronage firing, was still valid. But in 1990, just before Justice William Brennan retired, the Court extended the ban to hiring as well as firing, and for the first time in this vital area treated the applicant as well as the incumbent.[13] In other sectors the courts have also narrowed the gap between one who seeks and one who holds a government job.

Important differences remain, though, especially in the

realm of procedure. Often a statute will create a right to a hearing but will confine that right to people already in the workforce. When it comes to the Constitution, the basic rule is that a person may not be denied a job for reasons that would not justify a discharge. But for practical reasons the applicant may be less able than the incumbent to prove a violation of the Constitution. Rarely, for example, can an applicant demonstrate the degree of legal interest that would call for a hearing after a denial of initial employment. Thus, while the substantive rights are increasingly parallel, important differences remain in the ways those rights may be enforced.

### Do the rights of public employees apply off the job?

That depends very much on the nature of the job and on the policy or rule. Dress and uniform requirements typically stay at the workplace, though we will encounter one or two exceptions. When it comes to speech, the public worker may be freer to write critical letters to the editor from home than to protest agency policy at the office. On the other hand, if the workforce is to be tested for drugs or for diseases or for cholesterol levels, there is no way of separating on- and off-duty inquiry. And there are certain off-duty actions that may so directly and substantially affect relations on the job or the employee's effectiveness that governmental concern will carry over.

### May a public employee ever be forced to violate the rights of other people?

In general, no, though there are very few cases. Some years ago, the California Supreme Court held that a social worker could not be found insubordinate for refusing to violate what he believed to be the privacy rights of his clients.[14] Later a Detroit police officer won reinstatement after she was dismissed for refusing to pose as a prostitute or decoy—a role she argued was not only dangerous but constituted entrapment.[15] Schoolteachers could not be fired for continuing to send their children to a private school in violation of school policy. A Pennsylvania prison guard was upheld in his refusal to use force against a prisoner who had refused to "stand check" for religious reasons.[16] On the other hand, a devoutly Catholic FBI agent recently lost in court an analogous claim that he should not be required to conduct surveillance of antiwar groups.[17] So the picture remains mixed, with a majority of the few cases on this novel point seeming to favor the public worker who has reasonable grounds to object to being forced to abridge someone else's rights.

### What should a person do if he or she is denied employment on a seemingly improper ground?

A critical first step is to find out as much as one can about the reason for the rejection. Of course the reason (if any) that is given may not be the real reason but may be a mere pretext for action that really rests on other grounds. Thus the quest for the real reason, if sometimes elusive, is well worth pursuing.

When the reason is identified, some remedy may be readily apparent. If, for example, one has been rejected for reasons of gender or race (or both), the best bet may be to file a grievance with a state or local antidiscrimination agency. Such a complaint may also be taken to the federal Equal Employment Opportunity Commission, though the state or local remedy should be pursued first. (Chapter VI describes the functions and procedures of such agencies more fully.)

If the basis for the rejection is less clearly suspect, the procedures to be followed may also be less clear. Channels do not exist for the review of all types of adverse public employee actions; abridgements of free speech or political rights, for example, may need to be taken to court if there is no well-marked internal grievance path. Whatever the remedy, every effort should first be made to persuade the agency it acted improperly; should a judge later find that such an internal channel existed but was not pursued, that judge might dismiss a suit that has much merit simply because internal remedies were not fully exhausted before going to court.

### What should a public employee do if dismissed for a seemingly improper reason?

The status of the public worker who loses a job is somewhat different from that of the rejected applicant. Often there will be an established grievance procedure for incumbent employees. Resort to such a remedy is vital, even if the process is long and arduous, or if the employee is not very hopeful about its outcome. Going to court before pursuing all internal remedies may in the end prove counter productive. Sometimes the matter may be resolved through the internal channel, especially if the case was one of mistake or misunderstanding. If an internal appeal is unavailing, then the employee may seek outside recourse in much the same way as the rejected applicant.

If the discharge involved discrimination on grounds of race, gender, religion, age, disability, or national origin, the employee may seek external administrative review as soon as the internal procedures have been exhausted. Dismissal on other grounds may require the expert aid of a voluntary organization or an attorney or both.

**What relief is available to a person wrongly denied or dismissed from public employment?**

The most obvious and clearly most satisfactory relief is an order that the agency hire or rehire the complainant. Courts may also order the payment of money damages to a person who has been wronged, though the availability of such damages is not always clear. For example, it took until 1992 for the Supreme Court to recognize a private damage remedy for public employees injured by sex discrimination that violated Title IX of the Civil Rights Act[18]—nearly twenty years after the passage of the law.

In extreme cases, punitive damages (going beyond the actual losses that can be established by an injured public employee) may also be awarded. Other remedies, such as expunging or correcting an invalid file, may sometimes be even more valuable to the wronged employee than reinstatement or damages. Obviously the range of remedies will depend much on the nature of the case as well as the legal basis for relief.

## NOTES

1. *McAuliffe v. Mayor and Board of Aldermen*, 155 Mass. 216, 216, 29 N.E.2d 517, 517 (1892).
2. *Adler v. Board of Education*, 342 U.S. 485, 492 (1952).
3. *Keyishian v. Board of Regents*, 385 U.S. 589, 605–6 (1967).
4. *See, e.g.*, R. O'Neil, *The Price of Dependency* (1971); W. Van Alstyne, "The Demise of the Right-Privilege Distinction in Constitutional Law," 81 *Harv. L. Rev.* 1439 (1968).
5. *Rust v. Sullivan*, 114 L. Ed. 2d 233 (1991).

6.  *See infra* pp. 51–53.
7.  *See infra* pp. 14–15.
8.  *See infra* pp. 84–86.
9.  *See infra* pp. 73–76.
10. Washington Post, Aug. 10, 1992, at A17, cols 5–6.
11. *See infra* pp. 66–68.
12. *See, e.g., Foley v. Interactive Data Corp.*, 254 Cal. Rptr. 211, 765 P.2d 373 (1988). For a contrasting view, *see Schultz v. Industrial Coils, Inc.*, 125 Wis. 2d 520, 373 N.W.2d 74 (1985).
13. *Rutan v. Republican Party of Illinois*, 111 L. Ed. 2d 52 1990).
14. *Parrish v. Civil Service Commission*, 66 Cal. 2d 60, 425 P.2d 223, 57 Cal. Rptr. 623 (1967).
15. Detroit News, July 23, 1976, at 1F, col. 1.
16. *Harley v. Schuylkill County*, 476 F. Supp. 191 (E.D. Pa. 1979).
17. *Ryan v. United States Department of Justice*, 950 F.2d 458 (7th Cir. 1991).
18. *Franklin v. Gwinnett County*, 117 L. Ed. 2d 208 (1992).

# The Threshold of Public Employment: Initial Qualifications

Most people who seek work with a government agency probably assume they will be judged on their skills and merits. They are usually willing to take tests, if the job requires. They expect they may be asked certain questions, including a few that reach personal matters. They may also expect an inquiry into political belief or affiliation. But relatively few first-time applicants have a full sense of the extent to which the government may wish to know about their families as well as themselves or of the reach of public policy into their lives on and off the job. The initial threshold conditions, requirements, and inquiries are the subject of this chapter. (We defer to chapter V some closely related issues involving privacy interests of persons already employed.)

The government, as employer, often cares deeply about where its employees live (even ow long they have lived there), of what country they are citizens, whether they have ever been in trouble with the law, and myriad other matters such as age, height, weight, and other physical qualities. Most standards of this type bear some relationship to the governmental interests for which it employs people to carry out its responsibilities.

Yet other standards may not only bear tenuous relations to the public employer's needs but may create serious risks of abuse, discrimination, or invasion of the applicant's private and family life. The courts have therefore had to review such criteria with care and subjected them to constitutional standards that do not always readily carry over from other sectors. The uneasy and not always clear resolution of these disputes forms a fascinating part of the law of public employment.

## May state and local governments require United States citizenship as a condition of public employment?

Not as a general rule. In a nation that still has many first-generation migrants and descendants of recent immigrants, the issue is a critical one. In 1915 the Supreme Court had upheld citizenship requirements for public employment.[1] In the repressive period that followed many states used that precedent to deny employment to all noncitizens. Then in 1973 the High Court revisited the issue. New York State argued that it could reasonably keep aliens out of its civil service in order to ensure the loyalty of its workforce, and as a way of limiting tax-supported benefits to those persons most closely identified with government, as well as ensuring continuity of service by relaying upon citizens-employees.

The Supreme Court rejected all three of these arguments. In *Sugarman v. Dougall*,[2] the justices held the New York law (and similar bans of other states) to be in violation of the Fourteenth Amendment's Equal Protection Clause. While the Court recognized that a state might feel it important to exclude certain groups of aliens from especially sensitive jobs, that could only be done through "means . . . precisely drawn in light of the acknowledged purpose."[3] Not only had New York failed to do so; in fact, the state had actually hired aliens for some of the jobs that were more sensitive and strategic than were the jobs closed to noncitizens. The high Court left open the possibility that a state might "in an appropriately defined class of positions, require citizenship as a qualification for office,"[4] adding that "alienage itself is a factor that could reasonably be employed in defining 'political community.' "[5]

New York was among the first states to take advantage of that invitation. Two Empire State cases reached the Court in the mid 1970s, involving citizenship requirements for public-school teachers and for state troopers. The justices upheld both requirements, finding that citizenship was reasonably and specifically related to the state's needs in both occupations. For teachers, the Court stressed the state's need to ask its role models in the schools to make the commitment that citizenship reflected.[6] For troopers, it was the degree of discretion in enforcing "broad public policy" that the Court found a sufficient basis to bar aliens.[7]

A few years later, the justices also upheld California's refusal to hire aliens as probation officers.[8] The Court now reaffirmed the standard it had fashioned in the New York cases. Here it found that the duties of probation officers "sufficiently partake of the sovereign's power to exercise coercive force over the individual that they may be limited to citizens."[9]

Just as the exception seemed about to swallow the rule, the Supreme Court added a significant qualification. A 1984 case struck down a Texas law that required notaries public to be citizens.[10] The proper issue in testing such a policy, said the justices, was whether the "actual functioning of a position is such that the officeholder will necessarily exercise broad discretionary power over the formulation or execution of public policies importantly affecting the citizen population."[11] Commissioning notaries public did not meet that test.

There has been one other recent development. Georgia sought to limit certain jobs to native-born citizens. That, said a federal court in 1989, states may not do—not even for positions from which aliens might actually be barred.[12] Whatever the state's interest, native-born and naturalized citizens must be treated alike—probably for every position save that of President of the United States (for which the Constitution itself sets the standard).

## May citizenship be required for federal civil service positions?

After decades of uncertainty, the answer now seems to be yes. From the beginning of the federal civil service system in 1883, aliens were barred from classified federal jobs. Periodic court challenges were unavailing. Then in the 1976 case of *Hampton v. Mow Sun Wong*,[13] the Supreme Court ruled on quite narrow and technical grounds in favor of five lawfully resident aliens who had been rejected for federal positions. The justices concluded that these alien applicants had been denied due process because the Civil Service Commission's citizenship requirement had never been approved by the President or by Congress.

President Gerald Ford promptly amended the civil service rules to bar aliens from the federal service, except in very limited cases where their employment might be deemed essential to national interests.[14] The issue soon went back to the courts, which upheld the policy now that it had been properly adopted by Executive Order.[15] The United States government, in fact, possesses broader powers in this regard than do the states, since encouraging resident aliens to become citizens is a uniquely federal government role under our Constitution.

**May citizens be given a preference in public employment and public works?**

Probably not. Despite the deference of the courts to selective citizenship requirements, flat preferences have not fared well. Several lower federal courts have struck down such citizen preferences in regard to public works programs,[16] finding that in the allocation of public benefits aliens and citizens should be treated alike. The logic of such judgments seems clear: state government needs that might justify keeping aliens completely out of certain sensitive jobs would not apply at all, or with much lesser force, to a preference for citizen over noncitizen in a job for which either was qualified.

**May municipal employees be required to live within the city?**

Yes, almost certainly. In 1976 the Supreme Court held that a Philadelphia fireman named McCarthy could be dismissed because he had moved outside the city.[17] Earlier cases had distinguished between two seemingly similar prehiring tests—a requirement of *continuous* residency and a requirement of prior residency of a given duration. These cases had left open the validity of specific and uniformly applied residence standards. After the *McCarthy* case, lower courts elaborated the special governmental interests that such laws may serve. A federal appeals court, upholding a rule that required Cincinnati schoolteachers to live in the city, stressed among acceptable municipal goals a demonstrated commitment to an urban school system, closer contact with city government, greater familiarity with urban problems, and the need for a racially integrated workforce—all values the city might reasonably promote through a residence requirement.[18]

There are two recent and important qualifications to the general rule. Residence requirements may be suspect for quite different reasons. Take the case of a New Jersey suburb, 99.8 percent white, that insisted its employees live within its boundaries. The first black police officer the town hired balked at this requirement and brought suit claiming such a policy was racially discriminatory. Under the unusual conditions of the case, a federal judge agreed and exempted the minority officer.[19] The court noted that some of the town's valid interests might be served in other ways—for example, by requiring its minority workers to live within a certain distance, which would have tied them to their employer but would also have given them more residential options. One might note that the court did not strike down the residence requirement itself; presumably a white town employee could not have made a comparable claim.

The other recent development reminds us that applicants are different from people who are already employed. While cities may demand that their workers live where they work, a federal judge in Michigan ruled that municipalities may not flatly reject *applicants* who have not yet established residence.[20] If the person gets the job, a move may be necessary. But to force an applicant to relocate before seeking a position that may never be offered not only sets the price too high but exceeds the city's valid interest in wanting its workforce to live within its boundaries.

**May a city impose a waiting period for public employment?**

Probably not, though the Supreme Court has not spoken directly. The *McCarthy* case drew a distinction between tying the job to actual residence, on the one hand, and the use of a durational waiting period that the Court had struck down in other settings like welfare, medical care, and voting.[21] The city's legitimate interest is in *where* its employees live, not in *how long* they have been there. In fact several lower courts have struck down such waiting periods, which distinguish among lawful residents solely on the basis of time of arrival.[22] Unless the city can show that waiting periods serve some other interest, such a disability would not likely be sustained.

**May a city or state give preference in employment to its residents?**

Probably not, and for reasons similar to those that make waiting periods suspect. In 1978 the Supreme Court struck down an Alaska law that favored state residents in public works projects.[23] Though Alaska's goals were to reduce high unemployment and seasonal variations in the job market, the Court found the state's solution to be a clear breach of the Privileges and Immunities Clause of the Constitution. Several other courts have reached similar judgments in regard to public works preferences, suggesting that a direct employment preference would fare no better if it were challenged on similar grounds.

There is one caution. Recently a federal appeals court gave its blessing to a muted form of Alaska preference.[24] Wages of nonresident workers had been frozen until the differential between pay levels of residents and nonresidents matched or exceeded the cost-of-living gap between Alaska and Seattle. The court found that milder form of preference to be acceptable despite the earlier judgments striking down more blatant differentials. Preference might also be achieved by laws that require that a certain percentage of residents be employed on publicly funded projects—an approach that has fared better in the courts than has the flat or bald resident preference.

**May a public employee be forced to retire at a certain age?**

With few exceptions, forced retirement is no longer allowed. By broadening the Age Discrimination in Employment Act (ADEA) in 1986, Congress essentially uncapped mandatory retirement for virtually all public and private workers.[25] Two temporary exceptions survived for seven years—for police, fire officers, prison guards, and tenured university professors. Further study was called for in both cases. National commissions that were appointed separately to review the professorial and public safety caps have urged that the exceptions be allowed to expire in early 1993 when the grace period ends.[26]

Several narrow but important exceptions remain. One is for a small category of senior policymaking employees whose vested pension or benefits will be at least $44,000 annually at retirement.[27] Very few public officials will fall into this category, and most who do will actually be denied Age Discrimination protection for another and quite different reason, which follows.

Still subject to mandatory retirement are elected officials and those persons who are directly appointed by elected officials. The exemption applies to "persons elected to public office" and their personally appointed staffs and to "an appointee on the policy-making level or an immediate adviser with respect to the exercise of the constitutional or legal powers of the office."[28] Under this provision, the Supreme Court faced in 1991 the question whether Missouri could require its appointed state judges to retire at age seventy. Such a rule, the Court first held, was within the ADEA policymaking exemption, having been construed with proper respect for a state's judgments about how it wished to govern itself.

The justices then faced the constitutional issue of equal protection—an issue that had often been tested in earlier cases when mandatory retirement laws were pervasive and were uniformly upheld. The Court now held that Missouri might rationally choose seventy as an age at which to ask judges to step down—even though the state offered no proof of physical or mental deterioration by judges who reached that stage in life.[29] Such proof was not required under the quite lenient constitutional test the Court had earlier used to sustain mandatory retirement laws, and which applied here once the issue got beyond ADEA.

Thus judges, and perhaps other groups of senior policymaking appointed officials as well as elected officials, may still be forced to retire at a set age. On the other hand, a recent federal case reminds us this exception too has limits. The court declined to extend the statutory exemption any further than required, and specifically not to a third level of persons appointed by superiors who had in turn been appointed by elected officials.[30]

Finally, the Age Discrimination in Employment Act contains an exception for occupations and positions as to which age may be shown to be a bona fide occupational qualification. That test may be met, the courts have said, only by showing that the allegedly age-related job qualifications are essential to the normal operations of the agency; that age is "a necessary proxy for those job qualifications;" and that "all or substantially all people over a certain age would be unable to satisfy those job qualifications", or that individual testing for those job qualifications would be "impossible or highly impractical."

Despite the strong policy against age bias, a few courts have found these stringent tests to have been met by age limits that passed muster as bona fide occupational qualifications. The courts are divided on the question whether the first standard—the job-relatedness of age—may be invoked in the absence of generally enforced minimum standards for the particular qualification.[31]

**How does one establish a case under the Age Discrimination in Employment Act?**

Until 1974, the Act applied only to private employers. But now (with the few exceptions noted above) its protections apply fully to the public sector as will. It makes unlawful most age-based differential treatment of government employees over the age of forty. (The status of certain policies on age-related benefits is highly technical and remains an object of dispute between Congress and the courts.)

The scope and effect of the act must be qualified in two ways. For one, unlawful age discrimination may not be established, ipso facto, simply by showing an age differential between two persons. While courts are sympathetic to age-based claims, more is required to prove a case under the Act than showing that a younger person was hired for a position the plaintiff sought. Moreover, it is possible that seniority may still be invoked as a basis for personnel actions, even if age is to some degree implicated in those actions.

The other uncertainty concerns the definition of what is legally "discrimination." Not every age-based action or policy is forbidden. States and agencies may, for example, continue to establish "normal" retirement ages, so long as no coercive sanctions are used to enforce those norms. And quite recently, to illustrate the point in a different way, federal courts sustained a Massachusetts law that requires state employees over seventy to undergo annual physical examinations.[32] ADEA, in the federal judges' view, does not "limit employer-states' ability to assess the fitness of their employees."[33] That court found the physical exam, even though age-triggered, to be "a reasonable method to enable state employees to continue working while at the same time assuring their competency."[34] While potentially harmful age- based actions may be suspect under ADEA, not all are invalid.

**What remedies does the Age Discrimination Act provide?**

The Act includes such remedies as reinstatement of persons who have been unlawfully denied employment because of age. Earlier there was doubt about the availability of damages for pain and suffering and of punitive damages. Most federal courts seem now to have resolved that issue against allowing such damage claims; they have warned both of the potential for abuse and of the risk that unlimited damages might subvert the conciliation goals of the Act and its remedies.

## May a person be denied employment for being too young?

Many government positions set a certain minimum age. In a few states, the age discrimination laws have a lower floor than the forty-year threshold of the federal ADEA, even as low as eighteen. In such states a person between that statutory age and the minimum hiring age would presumably have a claim. Elsewhere the issue has turned on the recently lowered age of majority. New Jersey's Supreme Court held that if a person was old enough to vote, then he was also old enough to be a police officer, and on that basis struck down a provision that required an entrant to be at least twenty-one.[35] But other courts have taken a different view, and have generally sustained minimum-age laws. Recently a federal judge also upheld New York's twenty-one-year age rule for admission to the state bar.[36] The court stressed the importance of protecting the public—a rationale that would probably also apply to entry to government employment.

## May employment be denied to persons who do not meet minimum-height and minimum-weight standards?

Only when those standards are shown to be directly job-related. In 1977 the Supreme Court struck down an Alabama law that required all state prison guards to be at least five feet two inches in height, and to weigh at least one hundred twenty pounds.[37] The flaw in such a policy, said the Justices, was its clearly (if unintentionally) disproportionate effect on women. That decision was soon refined by lower federal courts, applying a two-level analysis: even if the statute or regulation is facially neutral with regard to gender (which would usually be the case), courts ask whether it nonetheless operates to discriminate against a protected class—women, Hispanic or Asian men, and the like. If so, most courts find the absence of any discriminatory intent immaterial.

Even before the courts intervened, many agencies were already in the process of eliminating or modifying such requirements. Most height limits had been established years ago, taking as the norm the average white-Anglo male. Dramatic changes in the demography of the workforce have drawn such norms increasingly into question and have caused public employers to question the wisdom and even the need for their continued use. Typical is the action of the United States Civil Service Commission in striking down both the minimum-height and minimum-weight limits for the National Park Police, absent proof of any correlation between such criteria and the demands of the job.[38]

**May an applicant be rejected for exceeding maximum weight limits?**

The answer may well depend on the position in question. Excess weight is clearly irrelevant to the vast range of tasks government workers are called upon to perform. Nor in most cases does being overweight, by itself, impair a public employee's health. Yet some government agencies, often for cosmetic reasons, set maximum-weight limits that are not job-related. Few antidiscrimination laws include size or weight among forbidden employment standards.

When these limits are challenged, courts have increasingly insisted upon close and precise correlation between weight and performance. Two contrasting California cases illustrate the analysis. One court held that a physical education teacher could not be discharged because her weight exceeded the school district's maximum, without clear proof that her size impaired her ability to teach.[39] On the other hand, a 1992 case upheld the suspension of a Los Angeles ambulance driver for having consistently surpassed the city's weight limits for its emergency personnel.[40]

Such reasoning has been applied in the surprisingly few other public employment cases, including a New York court's declaration that "obesity, standing alone, is not reasonably and rationally related to the ability to teach or to maintain discipline."[41] Most of the recent weight-limit cases have involved private employment; they have typically been resolved under employment discrimination statutes, often by finding (as with minimum-height limits) a disproportionate impact on women, as with upper-weight limits for airline flight attendants.

A contrary and insensitive approach persists, however. When a Florida fire department telephone operator sought reinstatement after being fired for being too heavy, the trial court ruled in her favor: "Her overweight does not have a deleterious effect upon her health or her ability to perform the job in question" and therefore was not disqualifying. But a state appeals court reversed, and the U.S. Supreme Court summarily affirmed.[42] Neither higher court insisted on judging the effect of weight upon performance.

## May an applicant be rejected solely because of a criminal record?

The answer depends very largely on the nature of the offense and to a lesser degree on the position being sought. Crimes obviously range from those that are severe and involve moral turpitude to those that are minor and technical in nature. The line of disqualification or government interest falls somewhere along that spectrum. Federal courts have consistently recognized that a traffic citation could not reasonably be used to deny a person public employment, though they caution that "a prior conviction of a serious offense would be a valid ground to disqualify a person from police work."[43]

Even where the crime may be more than technical—and far more serious than a traffic offense—courts have shown substantial clemency. The California Supreme Court, most notably, struck down a state law that denied a teaching credential to an otherwise fit person if the person had been convicted of a sex offense and had not received a "certificate of rehabilitation."[44] And occasional use of controlled substances, especially marijuana, has been treated much less harshly by courts reviewing employment qualifications than by employing agencies and rule-making bodies.[45]

The process and the factors are well illustrated by the fate of an Iowa law that forbade the employment of ex-felons in the state civil service. A federal judge found the law unconstitutional in a decision that set the standard for much that followed.[46] The court recognized that states may have several legitimate interests in limiting access of criminals to the public workforce but found the particular ban far broader than necessary to serve those interests.

Several features of this law especially troubled the court: it was extremely broad in scope and in fact created a conclusive and irrebuttable presumption based solely on the commission of a single felony at some time—no matter how far back—in the past. The court was also troubled by exceptions which undermined the fairness and rationality of the law; the legislature had actually exempted certain high level positions to which the concern about employing ex-felons ought to apply with particular force. Moreover, the line between felonies and misdemeanors has never been precise or uniform. Consequently, a person convicted of a misdemeanor that might centrally affect job status could be employable, while a merely technical and remote felony could be disabling.

Thus the Iowa federal court concluded: "[No] consideration is given to the nature and seriousness of the crime in relation to the job sought. The time elapsing since the conviction, the degree of the felon's rehabilitation, and the circumstances under which the crime was committed are similarly ignored."[47]

Other courts have generally followed this approach. There is a striking lack of judicial sympathy for laws that totally bar otherwise qualified felons from the civil service There are, however, a few cautions. If a state wishes to focus on a particular position and can demonstrate a close nexus between the crime (or all crimes) and the job, the outcome may be quite different. Thus a federal court quite recently sustained Rhode Island's refusal to hire convicted felons to drive school buses, noting that "it is difficult to imagine a more legitimate state interest than that of protecting vulnerable and impressionable school-age children from the possibility of either harm or immoral influences."[48]

Courts may also be readier to uphold a crime-based disability that is temporary than one that is permanent (for example, one that expires ten years after the crime and conviction). Thus, despite the general distaste of courts for crime-based employment bans, the ex-felon seeking government employment may still encounter occasional obstacles and will not invariably prevail in court.

### May a public employee or applicant object to the use of criminal records in judging eligibility?

The answer probably depends both on the nature of the position and on the applicable policy regarding the use and dissemination of criminal records. Occasionally the assessment of an applicant for a sensitive position may include a review of arrest records. But courts seem increasingly reluctant to permit wholesale inquiry into such files, and recent decisions suggest a diminishing level of acceptable government scrutiny of such records.

Meanwhile states have increasingly addressed this issue through legislation in different ways. Some states specifically allow arrest records to be sealed, and provide that an applicant for public employment need not disclose the contents of sealed records or even acknowledge their existence (since for application purposes they do not exist). Indeed, four or five states go even further and bar public as well as private employers from asking questions about, or using information concerning, arrests that did not result in convictions.[49]

Where records are sealed, the use of convictions as well as arrests may be excluded from the employment determination process. The trend seems to be toward such protections and safeguards, both with regard to arrest records as such and with regard to their use in making employment decisions. The differences among positions (and government interests in them) remains a critical factor. While crime-related disabilities diminish for most parts of the public workforce, the trend in the schools may (as the recent Rhode Island bus driver case suggests) be just the opposite.

## NOTES

1. *Heim v. McCall*, 239 U.S. 175 (1915).
2. 413 U.S. 634 (1973).
3. *Id.*
4. *Id.* at 647.
5. *Id.* at 649.
6. *Ambach v. Norwick*, 441 U.S. 68 (1979).
7. *Foley v. Connelie*, 435 U.S. 291 (1978). For a broad reading of these cases, *see, e.g.*, *Cervantes v. Guerra*, 651 F.2d 974 (5th Cir. 1981).
8. *Cabell v. Chavez-Salido*, 454 U.S. 432 (1982).
9. *Id.* at 445.
10. *Bernhal v. Faintner*, 467 U.S. 216 (1984).
11. *Id.* at 224.
12. *Fernandez v. Georgia*, 716 F. Supp. 1475 (M.D. Ga. 1989).
13. 426 U.S. 88 (1976).
14. Exec. Order No. 11935, 3 C.F.R. 146 (1976), *reprinted as amended in* 5 U.S.C. § 3301 (1988).

15. *Mow Sun Wong v. Hampton*, 435 F. Supp. 37 (N.D. Cal. 1977), *aff'd sub nom. Mow Sun Wong v. Campbell*, 626 F.2d 739 (9th Cir. 1980), *cert. denied sub nom. Lum v. Campbell*, 450 U.S. 959 (1981).

16. *C.D.R. Enterprises, Ltd. v. Board of Education*, 412 F. Supp. 1164 (S.D.N.Y. 1976), *aff'd sub nom. Lefkowitz v. C.D.R. Enterprises, Ltd.*, 429 U.S. 1031 (1977).

17. *McCarthy v. Philadelphia Civil Service Commission*, 424 U.S. 645 (1976).

18. *E.g., Brown v. New Haven Civil Service Board*, 474 F. Supp. 1256 (D. Conn. 1979); *Andre v. Board of Trustees of Maywood*, 561 F.2d 48 (7th Cir. 1977); *Fisher v. Reiser*, 610 F.2d 629 (9th Cir. 1979), *cert. denied*, 447 U.S. 930 (1980).

19. *NAACP, Newark Branch v. Harrison*, 749 F. Supp. 1327 (D.N.J. 1990).

20. *Grace v. City of Detroit*, 760 F. Supp. 646 (E.D. Mich. 1991).

21. *E.g., Shapiro v. Thompson*, 394 U.S. 618 (1969).

22. *Silver v. Garcia*, 760 F.2d 33 (1st Cir. 1985); *Grace v. City of Detroit*, 760 F. Supp. 646 (E.D. Mich. 1991); *cf. Bunyan v. Camacho*, 770 F.2d 773 (9th Cir. 1985).

23. *Hicklin v. Orbeck*, 437 U.S. 518 (1978). *See also United Building & Construction Trades Council v. Mayor of Camden*, 465 U.S. 208 (1984).

24. *International Organization of Masters, Mates and Pilots v. Andrews*, 831 F.2d 843 (9th Cir. 1987), *cert. denied*, 485 U.S. 962 (1988).

25. 29 U.S.C. §§ 621–634 (1988).

26. See National Academy of Sciences/National Research Council, Report of the Commission on the Uncapping of Mandatory Retirement for Tenured Faculty (1991); see report of study group on continuation of exemption for firefighters, police and prison guards, also recommending expiration, 30 Govt. Employment Relations Reporter No. 1448, p. 96 (1992).

27. 29 U.S.C. § 631(c)(1) (1988).

28. 29 U.S.C. § 630(f) (1988).

29. *Gregory v. Ashcroft*, 115 L. Ed. 2d 410 (1991).

30. *Id.* at 428.

31. *Id.* at 432.

32. *Tranello v. Frey*, 962 F.2d 244 (2d Cir. 1992).

33. *Compare, e.g., EEOC v. Kentucky State Police Department*, 860 F.2d 665 (6th Cir. 1988); *cert. denied*, 490 U.S. 1066 (1989); *EEOC v. Pennsylvania*, 829 F.2d 392 (3rd Cir. 1987), *cert. denied*, 485 U.S. 935 (1988); *with EEOC v. Mississippi State Tax Commission*, 873 F.2d 97 (5th Cir. 1989).

34. *EEOC v. Massachusetts*, 788 F.Supp. 106 (D. Mass. 1992).

35. *New Jersey State Police Benevolent Association v. Town of Morristown*, 65 N.J. 160, 320 A.2d 465 (1974). *But compare*, for contrasting views on similar issues, *Maine v. Duke*, 409 A.2d 1102 (Me. 1979); and *Stiles v. Blunt*, 912 F.2d 260 (8th Cir. 1990), *cert. denied*, 111 S. Ct. 1207 (1991).

36. *Baccus v. Karger*, 692 F. Supp. 290 (S.D.N.Y. 1988)

37. *Dothard v. Rawlinson*, 433 U.S. 321 (1977).

38. *Fox v. Washington*, 396 F. Supp. 504 (D.D.C. 1975).

39. *Blodgett v. Board of Trustees*, 20 Cal. App. 3d 183, 97 Cal. Rptr. 406 (1971).

40. *McMillen v. Civil Service Commission of the City of Los Angeles*, 6 Cal. App. 4th 125 (Cal. App. 1992). *See also Gray v. City of Florissant, Mo.*, 588 S.W.2d 722 (Mo. Ct. App. 1979).

41. *Parolisi v. Board of Examiners*, 55 Misc. 2d 546, 285 N.Y.S.2d 936 (1967).

42. *Metropolitan Dade County v. Wolf*, 274 So. 2d 584 (Fla. Dist. Ct. App. 1973), *cert. denied*, 414 U.S. 1116 (1974).

43. *United States v. City of Chicago*, 411 F. Supp. 218, 235 (N.D. Ill. 1976). *See also Dixon v. McMullen*, 527 F. Supp. 711 (N.D. Tex. 1981); and *see generally* N. Miller, "Criminal Convictions, 'Off Duty' Misconduct,' and Federal Employment: The Need for Better Definition of the Basis for Disciplinary Action," 39 *Am. U.L. Rev.* 869 (1990).

44. *Newland v. Board of Governors of California Community Colleges*, 566 P.2d 254 (Cal. 1977).

45. *Osterman v. Paulk*, 387 F. Supp. 669 (S.D. Fla. 1974). *But cf. Unzueta v. Ocean View School District*, 2d Civil No. B058873, 1992 Cal. App. LEXIS 714 (Cal. Ct. App. June 4, 1992), *modified and reh'g denied*, 1992 Cal. App. Lexis 828 (Cal. Ct. App. June 26, 1992).

46. *Butts v. Nichols*, 381 F. Supp. 573 (S.D. Iowa 1974).

47. 381 F. Supp. at 581.

48. *Hill v. Gill*, 703 F. Supp. 1034 (D.R.I. 1989), *aff'd without opinion*, 893 F.2d 1325 (1st Cir. 1989).

49. See Note, "*County of Milwaukee v. LIRC*: Levels of Abstraction and Employee Discrimination Because of Arrest and Conviction Records," 1988 *Wis. L. Rev.* 891.

# III

# Public Employment and Freedom of Speech

Speaking out can often get public employees into trouble. Government accountant A. Ernest Fitzgerald was fired for blowing the whistle on a multimillion-dollar cost overrun in production of the controversial C-5A transport.[1] A county key-punch operator in Texas named Ardith McPherson quipped after the 1981 attempt on President Reagan's life, "[I]f they go for him again, I hope they get him."[2] She lost her job the next day. Maryland prison guard Donald Hawkins was fired when he shouted at a bank teller he believed (erroneously) to be Jewish: "Hitler should have gotten rid of all you Jews."[3] A Texas school superintendent was suspended after he campaigned for one faction in a bitter school board election, and his faction lost.[4]

Each of these public workers went to court. In the end, all but one of them prevailed, though not without difficulty and substantial cost in time and money. Not every government employee who speaks out gets his or her job back. But, to paraphrase Justice Holmes's old maxim about the Boston policeman who was fired for getting involved in politics (and lost in court), the chances today of both keeping a government job and speaking out are far better than they were even a quarter century ago.

Retracing this arduous journey is the focus of this chapter. We begin with an issue that has been relatively quiet of late but provides important background—oaths of various kinds including loyalty oaths. We then move to the outspoken public employee and the newer controversies including those of whistle-blowers and other critics of government policy.

**May a public employee be required to take an oath of office?**
Yes. The Supreme Court held that the traditional oaths of office and of allegiance, long required of persons assuming many public positions, including the presidency of the United States, is constitutional.[5] The case involved a Massachusetts

law that required officeholders to swear (or affirm) that "I will uphold and defend the Constitution and laws of the United States and of the Commonwealth of Massachusetts and I will oppose the overthrow of the government by force, violence or by any illegal or unconstitutional means."[6] In sustaining this language, the Court stressed the historic role of oaths of allegiance, despite variations in the precise words. In an earlier case, the justices had noted that "the oath of constitutional support requires an individual assuming public responsibilities to affirm . . . that he will endeavor to perform his public duties lawfully."[7]

Mention of Massachusetts and oaths brings to mind a related issue. During the 1988 presidential campaign, there was a brief but intense debate between George Bush and Michael Dukakis on the question whether teachers in the Bay State could refuse to lead their class in saluting the flag and leading the pledge. In 1977, then Governor Dukakis sought an opinion of the state's highest court on a bill enacted by the legislature that would require teachers to lead the their students in the pledge of allegiance every morning. The court advised that such a law was constitutionally suspect.[8] Dukakis then vetoed the bill, setting in motion a highly charged issue that would end up in the presidential campaign a decade later.

Although the merits of the issue got lost along the way, there is a substantial difference between asking a teacher to swear a personal oath (which government may demand) and asking that same teacher, against conscience, to lead the class every morning in reciting the pledge. The Supreme Court has never ruled on this question, but the Massachusetts court's misgivings suggest the difficulty of the issue.

### May an oath concerning political belief be required?
In general, no oath broader than the oath of allegiance may be required of a person entering public employment. The Supreme Court has struck down several different kinds of oaths, either because their language was too vague and uncertain, or because they asked citizens to give up or surrender constitutional rights of free speech or belief. Such oaths have been both positive and negative in form. Of the positive type oaths, the Court in 1964 invalidated Washington's demand that its employees "will by precept and example promote respect for the

flag and [federal and state] institutions . . . , reverence for law and order and undivided allegiance to the . . . government."[9] The key to the judgment was the vagueness and breadth of the required commitment: "The teacher who refused to salute the flag or advocated refusal might well be accused of breaching his promise."[10] Since that case, few government agencies have sought to force their employees to make a positive commitment of loyalty broader than the Pledge of Allegiance.

Far more troublesome for free expression and thought have been negative, or disclaimer-type, oaths. Another part of the Washington law demanded that every applicant disavow being a "subversive person" or a member of a "subversive organization"—language not defined in the law, and which the Supreme Court also found unconstitutionally vague.

The Court very soon made even clearer its distaste for requiring a person to forswear membership in suspect or "subversive" groups. In striking down an Arizona law that barred from public employment anyone who would not disclaim membership in the Communist party or any other organization devoted to the overthrow of the government, the Court explained: "Those who join an organization but do not share its unlawful activities surely pose no threat, either as citizens or as public employees." Such a ban, the justices concluded, infringed on protected freedoms of expression and association, and "rests on the doctrine of 'guilt by association', which has no place here."[11]

What made these cases so striking in the 1960s was the vivid memory of an era, during the 1940s and 1950s, when thousands of government employees were in fact charged with "guilt by association" and lost their jobs not because of what they had done or threatened to do, but solely because of who their friends and colleagues were, or what groups they had joined, or even in some cases because they refused to protect themselves by accusing or implicating others. The demise of the disclaimer-type loyalty oath represents a dramatic shift in the role of the courts and in the law of free expression and government employment.

### Must an oath be precise and specific?
Even where government may have a valid basis for refusing to hire a person, the language used to disqualify is crucial. As we noted earlier, some of the early oath cases turned on the

vagueness or lack of clarity in the oath's language. The courts have said time and again that such imprecise language may force conscientious people to steer too wide a zone, and to avoid—or "chill" speech or association that is in fact constitutionally protected. Both people subject to such laws and the courts that review them need to know precisely what the lawmakers meant to require or forbid. Vague language in an oath clearly fails that standard.

### Can an oath be too precise or specific?

On the other hand, there is such a thing as being too precise. If the statute names a particular person or identifies an organization by name, it may then fail the constitutional test for quite a different reason. The Supreme Court in the 1960s struck down a law that made it criminal for an officer of the Communist party to hold office in a labor union.[12] While Congress may have had good reason to worry about Communist influence in organized labor, that goal could not be served by singling out and naming a group any more than by barring a named individual. Naming targets or suspects was what the framers had in mind when they forbade "Bills of Attainder." So an oath that focuses too narrowly on the target may be as suspect as one that sweeps too broadly.

### May an applicant be required to disavow membership in a specific organization (such as the Communist party)?

No, not unless the disclaimer or disavowal is limited to (1) active membership, (2) membership with knowledge of the illegal aims of the organization and (3) membership with the specific intent of furthering those unlawful aims.[13] Ordinary membership, even membership with knowledge of an unlawful goal, may not be proscribed—or made the basis for denying a government job. Thus a person who had joined the Communist party, or any other suspect group, for reasons other than overthrow of the government—civil rights, economic reform, or whatever—could not be disqualified on that basis.

After this basic framework was established, later cases saw applicants successfully challenge loyalty-type questions tied to federal employment. People seeking positions in the Veterans Administration had been required to indicate whether or not they belonged to the Communist party or any of its branches or subdivisions. They also had to tell whether at the time of application, or at any time within the previous ten years, they had belonged to a group that, to their knowledge, advocated the violent overthrow of the United States or of any state or local government. If an applicant responded affirmatively to the organizational question, he was then asked whether his membership reflected the specific intent to further the unlawful aims of the organization. If that question yielded an affirmative answer, the applicant then had to list the names of any such organizations, and the dates of his or her membership.

When this inquiry was challenged on constitutional grounds, the court held that it intruded unacceptably on the applicant's freedoms of speech and association.[14] Although the court conceded that government may keep out of public jobs people who are actively engaged in promoting its violent overthrow, such a risk cannot be presumed from membership in allegedly subversive groups. It must be directly established by means that are sensitive to due process as well as to free expression. Thus the loyalty questionnaire was found wanting in two respects under Supreme Court cases dealing with admission of allegedly subversive persons to the bar and their access to government benefits.

For one, the procedure for handling affirmative answers to the questions (and thereby avoiding an automatic disqualification) failed to afford due process. The other flaw was that an applicant could be penalized for active and knowing membership in an organization that merely taught or discussed the overthrow of the government but did not incite anyone to that goal. (Discussion and teaching are clearly protected by the First Amendment; only incitement that creates an immediate and grave danger to government may be punished or used to disqualify.)[15]

### May an applicant be required to forswear future political activity or affiliation?

No. Constitutional protection for what a person has done in the past or present applies with even greater force to the future. If questions about prior associations may chill protected activity, that risk is far greater when government seeks to deter future conduct or belief.[16] While in theory government could ask an applicant to forswear knowing, active membership in unlawful groups with the required specific intent, as a practical matter no rational agency would likely design a ban aimed at the only future activity government may constitutionally punish. Thus the issue is not likely to have much remaining significance.

In fact the whole subject has a rather ghostly quality at a time when, following the collapse of the Soviet Union, the Communist party is at greater risk in Russia than in the United States. The cold war pressures that created great anxiety and an elaborate loyalty-security system have now virtually abated. Indeed, that part of the world once dominated by communism seems about the only place where party membership would today place one at risk. Yet the history of witch-hunting and Red-baiting is still a recent and vivid enough memory in the United States and other western nations that we would be unwise to put it out of mind.

## May an applicant be required to list all organizations to which he or she belongs?

The answer depends on the scope and purpose of the inquiry. Some years ago the Supreme Court held that Arkansas could not require every teacher to compile a list each year of all the organizations to which he or she belonged.[17] Such a demand, said the Justices, went "far beyond what might be justified in the exercise of the State's legitimate inquiry into the fitness and competence of its teachers"[18] and threatened to deter teachers from perfectly lawful associations about which the state could have no valid concern. The Court implied that some teachers might be asked about some associations, and that government did have a valid interest in knowing about extracurricular commitments that might divert undue amounts of time from a teacher's primary tasks. But such interests could, if the state wished to pursue them, be served through much narrower and more precise inquiries.

The type of organization may also be relevant. Most such ties would fall either within the employee's zone of privacy (the subject of chapter V) or within the range of associations protected by the First Amendment—at least in so far as the organization is basically political in nature. The question how far beyond politics one's right to join may extend is a separate question we now address.

**Are nonpolitical associations also protected by the Constitution?**

For the most part, they seem to be. Nothing in the First Amendment limits freedom of association to political groups, even though most of the early history of First Amendment freedoms has involved such organizations. When the Baltimore Police Department rejected an applicant who had earned the top score on entrance exam because he admitted he belonged to a weekend nudist group, the issue was squarely posed. For several reasons, the court found in the applicant's favor. There was no indication he would refuse to wear clothes on the job or for that matter would have any difficulty in vigorously enforcing the laws against indecent exposure. Nor was there any evidence of unlawful activity on the part of the nudist organization. Thus the federal court held that the applicant's First Amendment freedoms included "the right to associate with any person of one's choosing for the purpose of advocating and promoting legitimate, albeit controversial, political, social and economic views."[19] The police commissioner had failed to demonstrate any governmental interest that outweighed the strong associational interest of an otherwise fully qualified applicant.

Since that case other courts have found in favor of nonpolitical associations on the part of public workers, refusing to confine freedom of association to familiarly political groups and causes. One federal appeals court, holding that a police officer could not be forced to stop dating the adopted daughter of a known mobster, dispensed entirely with the element of advocacy or cause that played some residual role in the nudist case. As this court observed in support of the policeman's constitutional claim: "The First Amendment freedom of association applies not only to situations where an advancing of common beliefs occurs, but also to purely social and personal associations."[20]

Recent cases further test and help to define the limits of free association. Another federal appeals court refused, for example, to reinstate a police officer fired for his off-duty association with a seventeen-year-old student. The agency's action reflected in part its concern about its own public image. But the court was also influenced by what it saw as a tenuous tie between the suspect association and traditional freedoms of expression—an association claim that seemed to the judges "too remote from the political rally, the press conference, the demonstration, the theater, or other familiar emporia of the marketplace of ideas to activate the guarantees of the First Amendment."[21] So what we know is that belonging to a nudist camp or similar nonpolitical group is almost certainly protected, and for familiar reasons; one holding so sensitive and visible a role in the public service as police officer may well enjoy less freedom of association than many fellow public employees.

## May a belief in God be required of public employees?

No. The precise question has not been decided, but the Supreme Court came close enough that we can safely infer such an answer. The justices held many years ago that Maryland could not require those who sought to be notaries public to swear that they believed in God as a condition of obtaining such a commission.[22] Under the religious freedom guarantees of the Constitution, the Court had long held that government may not discriminate on the basis of a person's religious belief —or lack of belief. Thus when a nonbeliever sought a notary public's commission, the Court was unanimous in finding that requirement in clear conflict with our nation's founding principles of religious liberty.

Any doubts about the role of religious liberty in choosing a public career were put to rest by a later Supreme Court judgment that states may not bar persons from holding public office because they are members of the clergy (as Tennessee had sought to do with its legislature.)[23] Indeed, until the Vatican required them to leave public office, two Roman Catholic priests served in Congress and a nun served as Michigan's commissioner of social services. Thus the relationship between religion and public employment seems to be one of complete neutrality, religious affiliation (or the lack of it) should neither help nor hinder a person seeking public office.

## Is a public employee free to protest or criticize government or agency policy?

The answer depends on many factors, and the reading of a number of cases that have defined (and refined) the applicable principles. In general, government workers enjoy the rights of citizens, including free speech. There are, however, special interests that come into play on both sides when a public employee speaks out critically about government or agency policy. On one hand, society benefits from permitting (indeed inviting) candor on the part of those most knowledgeable about how tax funds are being spent. On the other hand, government may have valid reasons for limiting or at least channeling such criticism.

Excessive controversy aired in public or in the press might impair the efficiency of an agency, the morale of its staff, or even the credibility it needs to serve its clientele. Moreover, government must appear neutral in ways that could be imperiled by outspoken staff members. There may also be certain kinds of information, not technically classified but highly sensitive, the effects of which may justify limits on the speech of those who possess such information.

The starting point for any legal analysis is the Supreme Court's 1968 decision in *Pickering v. Board of Education.*[24] The Court held that an Illinois public-school teacher could not be dismissed for statements he had made in the local media critical of school board policy without "proof of false statements knowingly and recklessly made."[25] Thus even though the teacher's comments contained some minor mistakes, they were not so far from the truth as to warrant his dismissal.

The Court stressed a number of factors that were to shape the law in later cases: there were no personal attacks on immediate superiors or fellow workers, only a general critique of agency policy. The statements had been prepared by the teacher on his own time, with no use of school facilities. While a teacher is presumed to know something about school board policy and operations, these were not the highly damaging revelations of an expert or insider, nor did they disclose any secret or confidential information. For these and other reasons the Court found *Pickering* itself an easy case in which to apply the new standard in the public employee's favor. The decision left, however, many issues that were to be the focus of hundreds of later cases.

## How does the subject matter affect the public employee's right to speak out?

The central element is that the information must address a matter of "public importance" or "public concern" before it invokes the *Pickering* test. The Supreme Court stressed this element when it revisited the issue in *Connnick v. Myers*[26] in

1983. An assistant district attorney in Louisiana had circulated to her colleagues and co-workers a questionnaire asking about office morale, transfer policy, the level of confidence in supervisors, the need for a grievance policy, and whether others felt pressured to take part in political campaigns. She was terminated, in part because the questionnaire was seen as an act of insubordination.

The discharged attorney brought suit, claiming her dismissal abridged free speech under the *Pickering* doctrine. But a Supreme Court majority disagreed, finding that with one exception, "these questions reflect one employee's dissatisfaction with a transfer and an attempt to turn that displeasure into a cause célèbre." Elsewhere the Court found the survey to be "an employee grievance concerning internal office policy." Since the "public concern" standard had not been met, there was no need to pursue the rest of the *Pickering* inquiry.

Later cases in the lower courts have struggled with *Connick's* limitation on the "public concern" standard. Clearly where a public employee is asked to give testimony before a legislative body or to file an official report in the line of duty, any critical comments about an agency policy or a superior are likely to be viewed as matters of "public concern."[27] On the other hand, when a government employee "speaks as an employee on matters that address his personal employment conditions," most courts do not find a matter of public concern but only a private issue.[28] Yet the presence of a personal stake or interest does not automatically deny First Amendment protection if the issue being raised has broader import; observed one federal court of appeals in finding "public concern" in just such a case, "the employee did not merely claim that she was being mistreated— she claimed that she was the victim of retaliation arising out of racial animus within the state police. This is a matter of public concern."[29]

Some of the most difficult cases arise in the realm of politics, where a public official runs afoul of contending forces on the board or agency to which he reports. In one such recent case, a Texas school superintendent became involved in a public contest among members of his board. When his faction lost, the group he had opposed removed him, claiming that his intervention had been not only unwise but disruptive and personal rather than professional in nature. But the federal appeals court backed the superintendent, finding an arena of public concern in the issues he had raised and the role he played.[30] Others in similar circumstances have fared less well. This is an area into which the public worker ventures at some peril and with no assurance that *Pickering* protection will always avail.

The public concern standard thus becomes elusive and variable. The *Connick* Court recognized the difficulty of framing neat and simple rules: "Whether an employee's speech addresses matters of public concern must be determined by the content, form and context of a given statement, as revealed by the whole record."[31] Yet the determination is not simply a judgment of fact for trial courts or juries to make. It is a matter of profound constitutional importance for outspoken government employees. Most important, it is the threshold question that must be first addressed before the *Pickering* analysis proceeds.

## What bearing does *Pickering* have on outspoken public employees whose speech is not protest or criticism?

The issue emerged recently in a most unusual context—a police officer who owned a quarter interest in a video store that rented a few nonobscene adult films, though most of its fare was less controversial. The department reprimanded the officer for "unbecoming conduct" and for having failed to obtain approval for his moonlighting. The officer went to federal court and eventually prevailed on free speech grounds.[32] The court recognized his activity was clearly speech and was fully protected on First Amendment grounds. His public employee status, however, complicated the analysis, and this was not the kind of case in which a "public concern" finding was really germane. While the *Pickering-Connick* principles did not literally apply to a nonprotest speech situation, they did furnish an analogous framework.

The court then balanced the contending interests of police force and officer, in familiar *Pickering* fashion. That balance brought about a vindication of the officer despite possible public criticism of the department. The court's conclusion is striking: "Although the officer's speech may not be as 'valuable' as political or social conduct, we think that this type of off-duty public employee speech must be accorded the same weight that would be accorded comparable expression by citizens who do not work for the state."[33] Of course not every court would read

*Pickering* so broadly, though others might well reach the same result by different paths.

## What bearing do the internal needs of the agency have on the scope of a public worker's protest?

From the start, courts have warned that some public employee speech may so adversely affect the agency as to warrant discipline. Thus one of the survey questions the *Connick* court judged separately and apart from the "public concern" issue—whether staff members had confidence in, and relied on, the word of five named supervisors—failed by that standard as well: because "close working relationships are essential to fulfilling public responsibilities" in such an agency, this question "is a statement that carries the clear potential for undermining office relations."[34] Other courts have recognized as a key factor the risk that employee speech may impair agency morale or otherwise jeopardize the internal working of the agency, especially when close collaboration among professionals is needed.

In such cases, potential harm may be inferred without awaiting the results. The *Connick* Court cautioned: "We do not see the necessity for an employer to allow events to unfold to the extent that the disruption of the office and the destruction of working relationships is manifest before taking action."[35]

The Supreme Court did, however, make clear in a later case that this canon must be sparingly applied. When Texas county clerical worker Ardith McPherson remarked to fellow employees after the 1981 attempt on President Reagan's life, "[I]f they go for him again, I hope they get him," she was discharged. She brought suit in federal court, and eventually won a close Supreme Court decision.[36]

After finding the subject of her remark to be clearly a matter of "public concern" despite its provocative tone, the Court addressed the agency's central claim of harm to internal morale and efficiency. Though the statement had been made at the workplace and was heard by some co-workers, "there is no evidence that it interfered with the efficient functioning of the office." The Court found several factors helpful in reaching that conclusion—among them evidence that "McPherson's discharge [was] unrelated to the functioning of the office," and that the constable (her boss) did not even try to find out which fellow employees had heard the statement.[37]

### Does the role or position of the speaker within the agency matter?

It does matter, and in three ways. One dimension is simply the level of the position within the agency. Clearly statements by some people will have far greater effect both internally and externally than others. Here again the *McPherson* case is instructive. The Court stressed that "some attention must be paid to the responsibilities of the employee within the agency," taking note of the low level and nonsensitive role of a clerical worker in a county constable's office, along with the complete lack of any policymaking duties or confidential tasks. Moreover, and crucial to this judgment, it was clear McPherson did not have (and likely would not have in the future) any responsibility for the agency's primary and sensitive law enforcement tasks.

A second dimension is one we noted earlier—the personal dynamics within the agency and the degree to which personal loyalty would be expected. The *Pickering* Court suggested attention to "positions in public employment in which the relationship between superior and subordinate would seriously undermine the effectiveness of the working relationship," though no such risk existed in *Pickering* itself. Later cases stressed the effect of critical speech upon just such relationships of trust and confidence, and sustained adverse personnel actions for speech that would surely have been tolerable from a less sensitively placed or more remote public worker.[38]

The third dimension is the relationship of the speaker to the source of the information. Curiously, this factor can cut both ways. The *Pickering* Court suggested that the result in that case might have been different if "a teacher has carelessly made statements about matters so closely related to the day-to-day operations of the schools and any harmful impact on the public would be difficult to counter because of the teacher's presumed access to the real facts."[39] It is clear that when someone speaks as a nonexpert, the risk of harm (e.g., misleading others) is lower than when the criticism comes from someone close to the source or in possession of strategic information.

Yet there may be a countervailing interest—that of encouraging the greatest degree of candor from those best positioned to know the truth, people from whom society has the keenest interest in learning the truth. Moreover, the degree of "public concern" usually varies inversely with the distance between the speaker and the source of knowledge. Thus there are no clear and simple rules about the "expertise" issue; some courts will grant greatest protection to the expert, while others will hold the expert to a higher standard of accuracy than other public workers. Both approaches seem consistent with the policies of *Pickering* and its progeny, though occasionally confusing in the quest for guidance.

### May the external perception of the speech affect the scope of the employee's rights?

Clearly the agency's interests include its ability to serve its clients and its mission. As the *McPherson* Court noted, an outspoken employee can jeopardize that capacity—as, for example, might well have been the case if the "I hope they get him" remark had been made by a uniformed officer within hearing of citizens who look to such a person for impartial law enforcement and justice. Courts recognize a concern that public employee speech may impair an agency's impartiality or neutrality—as in the case of a San Francisco social worker asked to take down an office poster that conveyed a possibly biased political message. In such cases, judges rightly defer to agency concerns about the external impact of such statements and expressive activity.[40]

### Is the tone of the employee speech relevant?

Yes, although the *McPherson* case reminds us that public workers must be allowed to use fairly strong language. The reason for such latitude is best explained by a New York court that warned that the limits could be so narrow that "those who criticize in any area where criticism is permissible would either be discouraged from exercising their right or would do so in such innocuous terms as would make the criticism seem ineffective or obsequious."[41] Some courts have sanctioned the use by public workers of fairly strong language, guided by just such perceptions. There are a few exceptions—cases in which the tone of the message has played a part in the outcome—as with a Canal Zone police officer some years ago who wrote a poem the court called "an intemperate lampoon," accompanied by a letter that showed a "contemptuous quality,"[42] or a Connecticut teacher whose discharge was sustained partly because of the acid tone and vicious language in which he couched his criticism of superiors.[43]

## What if the public employee's speech offends on grounds of race, gender, religion, or ethnic group?

Here the courts have been surprisingly inconsistent in applying the *Pickering* standard. In several cases, dismissals for such remarks were simply sustained without reference to the constitutional tests—as in the case of a Florida dietician who confronted a Jewish co-worker with the claim "you know about Jews . . . they are all pushy and aggressive"[44] or the white Nebraska teacher who asked his racially mixed class, "How many times a day do I have to ask you dumb niggers to stop playing around?"[45] or the Minneapolis building inspector who remarked of sanitary conditions in the city's Native American sector, "they used to be able to crap all over the place and move the tepee; they can't do that any more."[46]

Two recent Maryland cases, one federal and the other state, recognize the need to apply *Pickering* principles consistently to such cases. The earlier case concerned veteran white Baltimore police officer Bobby Berger, whose evening and weekend avocation was performing an Al Jolson routine in blackface. Though never identified as an officer, Berger was enough of a celebrity that his occupation was seldom a secret, and he became known in the media as "the singing cop." After protests from leaders of the black community, police officials ordered Berger to abandon his routine. When he refused, discipline was imposed. Berger took the case to a federal court, claiming an abridgment of his freedom of expression.

The court of appeals ruled in his favor.[47] Despite the novelty of the issue, the court applied the full *Pickering* framework— first by finding the performances to be matters of "public concern", even though the context was entertainment rather than politics. The court then balanced contending interests—on one hand, the department's undoubted interest in maintaining good community relations, and in preventing the disruption that Berger's critics had threatened—but concluded that such fears did not justify stifling expressive conduct of this novel variety. People who found Berger's routine offensive had the remedy of protesting on their own and need not invoke the internal sanctions of the police department.

The later case provides a valuable contrast, since it came from the same locale but went through the state court system.[48] A Maryland prison guard named Hawkins confronted a bank teller whom he erroneously believed to be Jewish: "Hitler should have gotten rid of all you Jews."[49] Like *Berger*, the incident occurred away from the job site and off duty. And like *Berger*, the expression was highly offensive to at least one ethnic group. But there the cases differed. Hawkins's speech reflected little of public concern: "the officer's uncontrolled urge verbally to abuse [the teller] was purely personal"[50] and had nothing to do, for example, with starting "a dialogue on the Holocaust."[51]

Thus the public concern test simply did not apply, and the substantial interests of the agency—"apprehension of disruption and possible physical violence at the institution"—sufficed to sustain Hawkins's discharge. Moreover, an employee who once flew off the handle on such minor provocation might "resort to ethnic or racial abuse if frustrated under the considerable pressures of attempting to maintain order in a penal institution"—a timely reminder that the employee's role and responsibilities always enter the equation in such cases.

### Is the amount of time devoted to employee speech a factor?

Yes, if it becomes substantial and takes time away from the job, or dilutes the employee's primary task. Most of the cases we have noted here involved either off-duty activity or instantaneous speech at the workplace. But there is always the possibility that time may become a concern. There was, for example, the case of a University of North Carolina faculty member who canceled a class to express his views on national policy away from the campus. Even though his speech was clearly protected by the First Amendment, the court sustained a nonrenewal of his appointment, noting "that the failure to carry out his responsibility . . . was because he was elsewhere exercising his right of free expression does not excuse his unwillingness to perform those duties which he had undertaken."[52] Such cases are relatively rare, but the government interest in getting a full day from its employees is nonetheless substantial.

### May an employee be required to "clear" speech or protest through agency channels?

The *Pickering* case left open the question of "how far teachers can be required by narrowly drawn grievance procedures to submit complaints about the operation of the schools to their superiors before bringing the complaints before the public."[53] Early post-*Pickering* cases seemed unsympathetic to such clearance rules—one court striking down such a requirement because it was vague and had not been consistently applied;[54] another because the agency could show no "impairment of the public service" from the failure to follow channels;[55] and the third because the procedure would have barred an employee from taking his concern directly to the cabinet officer who headed his agency.[56]

Later cases have shown greater deference to clearance rules. Illustrative is the case of an Internal Revenue Service attorney who unsuccessfully sought reinstatement after he was fired for filing a class action on behalf of a religious group without obtaining the permission that IRS policy required. In upholding the sanction, the court of appeals stressed the agency's interest in requiring clearance so as, among other interests, to avoid actions that might imply impropriety on the part of agency lawyers.[57] Moreover, the court felt such an approval procedure imposed only an incidental burden on the attorney's outside expressive activities. The result in such cases will continue to depend both on the nature of the clearance and review process, and on the impact that compliance may have on a public worker's right to speak out on matters of public importance.

The Supreme Court has addressed a closely related issue—the degree to which a public employee may be bound, following retirement, by an agreement not to write about job experiences. Frank Snepp left the Central Intelligence Agency, where he had signed an agreement not to publish anything about the agency during or after his employment there. He then proceeded to write a book about his activities in Vietnam. Though he did not use any classified information, the CIA nonetheless sought to impose, under the agreement Snepp had signed, a "constructive trust" on the proceeds from the book. When the case reached the Supreme Court, a majority upheld the CIA's claim and enforced Snepp's commitment as a contractual obligation, without even mentioning free speech issues.[58] Only the dissenters hinted there might be free speech problems, and even they confined that concern to the CIA's attempt to limit Snepp's use of unclassified information.

In the post-*Snepp* era, there have been several other skirmishes over postemployment publication in violation of agreements signed by a former government employee. The general willingness of courts to enforce such obligations gives further force to relatively routine clearance requirements—especially where (as would usually be the case) they form part of the initial employment agreement or understanding.

## Can government insist its employees speak only English on the job?

No. Arizona amended its constitution in 1988 to mandate English as the only official language of the state. All public employees were forbidden to use any other language on the job. A group of Hispanic state employees sued in federal court, claiming the amendment denied them freedom of speech, and they prevailed. The court found the case a relatively easy one. The scope of the amendment was so broad that it would, for example, have barred a legislator from speaking with constituents in a non-English tongue or a judge from performing a marriage ceremony in any other language. Since the First Amendment clearly gives those employees a right to converse other than in English, Arizona's attempt at homogeneity and linguistic uniformity failed the most basic of constitutional tests.[59] The district court judgment was never appealed and seems to settle the issue in the public sector—though private employers seem to be making increased use of English-only rules.

There has been recent and related concern over the accents of nonnative teachers. One Massachusetts city contemplated, but quickly withdrew, a proposal to bar persons with foreign accents from teaching elementary school classes. While the ban was being debated, the state's attorney general expressed strong opposition and threatened to sue the city under the civil rights laws should such a measure be adopted.[60] Several months earlier, the United States Equal Employment Opportunity Commission did in fact file suit against a private employer for having fired an Indian-born employee because of his accent.[61]

## Can government bar its employees from speaking or writing for pay?

That may depend on the nature of the ban. In the Ethics Reform Act of 1989,[62] Congress attempted to do just that.

Reflecting a desire to promote integrity in the public workforce, this law forbade virtually all federal employees from accepting any honoraria for giving speeches or writing books or papers, even on their own time and on subjects remote from their jobs. The ban aroused immediate indignation within the federal service and would have imposed serious hardship on many prolific writers within the government. Suit was brought, and in March 1992, a district judge struck down this ban[63]—not because Congress lacked the constitutional power to prevent conflicts of interest or improprieties (or the appearance thereof), but because this law reached far beyond such interests. Honoraria were banned "even when there is neither the possibility nor a perception that the office and the payment are interdependent." This judgment was affirmed by the federal court of appeals in late March 1993.

The district court also noted how the law singled out certain speeches and writings—the core First Amendment pursuits—while leaving alone many other equally or less expressive activities. Thus the Act, despite its laudable aim, turned out to be both too broad in one sense and too narrow in another. A more precise restriction on certain kinds of payments may well replace this law at some later time, matching more closely the narrow ethical constraints already imposed on judges and certain other categories of government employees.

### What protection exists for "whistle-blowers" in government?

Some of the cases we noted earlier provide protection to people like Pickering and others whose right to criticize government policy or personnel is now substantially ensured by the First Amendment. Yet there is a need for separate procedures and provisions to address the special plight of the genuine whistle-blower. And courts have shown themselves increasingly sympathetic to the courageous employee who risks status and even livelihood to expose wrongdoing—as witness the $7.5 million judgment recovered in the summer of 1992 by a former employee of a military contractor who revealed how his company had defrauded the Pentagon.[64] Judgments in the public sector may be smaller, though note should be taken of the $50,000 a federal jury ordered the former manager of New York's transit system to pay from his own pocket to a subway conductor he fired after the conductor publicly revealed serious safety problems.[65] While the stakes are high on the individual's side, the successful whistle-blower may in the end reap handsome rewards.

Many specific provisions in federal and state law offer some protection to whistle-blowers within particular agencies or branches of government. In 1978 Congress adopted a new policy and procedure to protect federal whistle-blowers, and created an Office of Special Counsel for that purpose.[66] But by the mid 1980s, little had been done to implement or invoke that law. Concerned members of Congress claimed there had not been a single case in which the Special Counsel took action to restore the job of any discharged whistle-blower. Thus efforts began for a new and more comprehensive whistle-blower protection law, which passed both houses of Congress in 1988— only to be pocket-vetoed by President Reagan because of concerns about an executive office not subject to presidential control.

Shortly before leaving office, Reagan offered a modified approach to whistle-blower protection. The new legislation overwhelmingly passed both houses of Congress and was signed into law by President George Bush as the Whistle Blower Protection Act of 1989.[67] The new statute makes it easier for whistle-blowers to prove their cases, and at the same time increases the burden for federal agencies defending against whistle-blowing claims.

There are other important innovations. Whistle-blowers may for the first time go to court to appeal their own cases. The new law also enhances the safeguards of confidentiality. The major structural change is in strengthening and sharpening the investigative and protective powers in the enhanced Office of the the Special Counsel—now made an independent agency, no longer empowered to oppose whistle-blowers before the Merit Systems Protection Board or in court, but at the same time forbidden to bring suit against other government agencies on behalf of whistle blowers.

It is still too early to know just how well the new law will serve the needs of whistle-blowers. The first major test of the Act did not occur until the spring of 1992. It resulted initially in the reinstatement of Defense Department scientist Aldric Saucier, who had been fired for exposing waste and fraud in the Strategic Defense Initiative (Star Wars) program. But after the Defense Department had agreed to the reinstatement, the Office of Special Counsel announced it was closing the case because Saucier had demanded that certain information he had supplied not be given to the Defense Department.[68] Thus the first major test of the new law came to little—though the initial reinstatement suggests at least a partial victory that might not have occurred without the heightened protections that Congress created in 1989. More cases will be needed to define the scope and value of the new approach.

## NOTES

1. *See* A. Ernest Fitzgerald, "Blowing the Whistle on the Pentagon," in Norman Dorsen and Stephen Gillers, eds., *None of Your Business: Government Secrecy in America*, 251–77 (1974); New York Times, Sept. 19, 1973, at 1, cols. 6–7; Oct. 4, 1973, at 51, col. 4.

2. *Rankin v. McPherson*, 483 U.S. 378, 381 (1987).

3. *Hawkins v. Department of Correctional Services*, 602 A.2d 712, 713 (Md. 1992).

4. *Kinsey v. Salado Independent School District*, 950 F.2d 988 (5th Cir. 1992).

5. *Cole v. Richardson*, 405 U.S. 676 (1972).

6. Mass. Gen. Laws ch. 264, § 14.

7. *Law Students Research Council v. Wadmond*, 401 U.S. 154, 192 (Marshall, J., dissenting); *see also Knight v. Board of Regents*, 269 F. Supp. 339 (S.D.N.Y. 1967), *aff'd*, 390 U.S. 36 (1968).

8. *Opinion of the Justices to the Governor*, 372 Mass. 874, 363 N.E.2d 251 (1977).

9. *Baggett v. Bullitt*, 377 U.S. 360, 362 (1964).

10. 377 U.S. at 371.

11. *Elfbrandt v. Russell*, 384 U.S. 11, 19 (1966).

12. *United States v. Brown*, 381 U.S. 437 (1965).

13. *Scales v. United States*, 367 U.S. 203 (1961).

14. *Shapiro v. Roudebush*, 413 F. Supp. 1177 (D. Mass. 1976).

15. *Brandenburg v. Ohio*, 395 U.S. 444 (1969).

16. *See Keyishian v. Board of Regents*, 385 U.S. 589 (1967).

17. *Shelton v. Tucker*, 364 U.S. 479 (1960).

18. *Id.* at 490.

19. *Bruns v. Pomerlau*, 319 F. Supp. 58 (D. Md. 1970); *see also McKenna v. Peekskill Housing Authority*, 497 F. Supp. 1217 (S.D.N.Y. 1980), *aff'd in part*, 647 F.2d 332 (2d Cir. 1981).

20. *Wilson v. Taylor*, 733 F.2d 1539 (11th Cir. 1984).

21. *Swank v. Smart*, 898 F.2d 1247 (7th Cir.), *cert. denied*, 111 S. Ct. 147 (1990).

22. *Torcaso v. Watkins*, 367 U.S. 488 (1961).

23. *McDaniel v. Paty*, 435 U.S. 618 (1978).

24. 391 U.S. 563 (1968).

25. *Id.* at 574.

26. 461 U.S. 138 (1983).

27. *See, e.g., Piesco v. New York City Department of Personnel*, 933 F.2d 1149 (2d Cir. 1991); *Koch v. City of Hutchinson*, 814 F.2d 1489 (10th Cir. 1987), *aff'd on reh'g en banc*, 847 F.2d 1436 (10th Cir. 1988), *cert. denied*, 488 U.S. 908 (1988).

28. *See, e.g., Stewart v. Parish of Jefferson*, 951 F.2d 681 (5th Cir. 1992), *cert. denied*, 1992 U.S. LEXIS 5638 (1992).

29. *Rode v. Dellarciprete*, 845 F.2d 1195, 1201 (3d Cir. 1988).

30. *Kinsey v. Salado Independent School District*, 950 F.2d 988 (5th Cir. 1992).

31. *Connick v. Meyers*, 461 U.S. 138, 147–48 (1983).

32. *Flanagan v. Munger*, 890 F.2d 1557 (10th Cir. 1989).

33. Id. at 1565–66.

34. 461 U.S. at 151–52.

35. 461 U.S. at 168.

36. *Rankin v. McPherson*, 483 U.S. 378 (1978).

37. 483 U.S. at 389.

38. *See, e.g., Berg v. Hunter*, 854 F.2d 238, 244 (7th Cir. 1988).

39. 391 U.S. at 572.

40. *E.g., Phillips v. Adult Probation Department of City and County of San Francisco*, 491 F.2d 951 (9th Cir. 1974); *Allen v. Lewis-Clark State College*, 105 Idaho 447, 670 P.2d 854 (1983).

41. *Puentes v. Board of Education*, 24 N.Y.2d 996, 999, 250 N.E.2d 232, 233, 302 N.Y.S.2d 824, 826 (1969).

42. *Meehan v. Macy*, 392 F.2d 822, 836 (D.C. Cir. 1968).

43. *Gilbertson v. McAllister*, 403 F. Supp. 1 (D. Conn. 1975).

44. *Cowell v. Fuller*, 362 So. 2d 124, 125 (Fla. Dist. Ct. App. 1978).

45. *Clarke v. Board of Education of the School District of Omaha*, 338 N.W.2d 272, 273 (Neb. 1983).

46. *Thompson v. Minneapolis*, 300 N.W.2d 763, 765 (Minn. 1980).

47. *Berger v. Battaglia*, 779 F.2d 992 (4th Cir. 1985).

48. *Hawkins v. Department of Public Safety and Correctional Services*, 602 A.2d 712 (Md. 1992).

49. *Id.* at 713.

50. *Id.* at 720.

51. *Id.* at 717.

52.  *Blevins v. University of North Carolina*, No. C–21- D–70 (M.D.N.C. Sept. 8, 1971).

53.  391 U.S. at 512 n.4.

54.  *Meehan v. Macy*, 392 F.2d 822 (D.C. Cir. 1968); *cf. Huff v. Secretary of the Navy*, 413 F. Supp. 863 (D.D.C. 1976).

55.  *Klein v. Civil Service Commission*, 260 Iowa 1147, 152 N.W.2d 195, 201 (1967).

56.  *Swaaley v. United States*, 376 F.2d 857 (2d Cir. 1967).

57.  *Williams v. Internal Revenue Service*, 919 F.2d 745 (D.C. Cir. 1991).

58.  *Snepp v. United States*, 444 U.S. 507 (1980).

59.  *Yniguez v. Mofford*, 730 F. Supp. 309 (D. Ariz. 1990).

60.  See New York Times, July 5, 1992, sec. 1, at 12, cols. 5–6.

61.  New York Times, Jan. 18, 1992, at 9, cols. 4–6.

62.  Pub. L. No. 95–454, § 202(a), § 1206, 92 Stat. 1125 (1978), 5 U.S.C. § 1206 (1988).

63.  *National Treasury Employees Union v. United States*, 788 F. Supp. 4 (D.D.C. 1992), *aff'd*, 61 U.S.L. Week 2591 (D.C. Cir. Mar. 30, 1993).

64.  New York Times, July 15, 1992, at A1, col. 2.

65.  Washington Post, June 24, 1991, at D1, cols. 2–3.

66.  Pub. L. No. 95–454, 92 Stat. 1111 (1978) (codified in scattered sections of 5 U.S.C.).

67.  Pub. L. No. 101–12, 103 Stat. 16 (1988) (codified in scattered sections of 5 U.S.C.).

68.  Washington Post, Mar. 7, 1992, at A8, cols. 1–3, May 13, 1992, at A6, cols. 5–6.

# IV

# Politics, Patronage, Public Service, and Unions

June 21, 1990, was a most important day in shaping the role of politics in the public service. By pure coincidence, just a few hours apart and a few hundred yards away, Congress and the Supreme Court both took actions of the utmost significance for millions of government employees across the nation.

The United States Congress on that day ended a three-year-long quest to broaden the range of political activity in which federal workers may take part. By the thinnest of margins, the Senate sustained President Bush's veto of a bill that would have dramatically relaxed the curbs Congress had imposed fifty years earlier in the Hatch Act.[1] Like several of his predecessors who strongly opposed any effort to weaken the Hatch Act's wall between politics and civil service, Bush had promised to veto the bill. He then made the veto a test of his leadership of the civil service. Since the House of Representatives had already overriden the veto, the Senate action was crucial. By two votes, the override attempt failed. The Hatch Act thus ended its first half-century intact.

On the very same day, just across the street, Justice William Brennan delivered what was to be his final major First Amendment opinion. By a 5–4 margin, the Court held that virtually any use of party affiliation (or lack of it) to judge or place public employees violated the Constitution's guarantees of free speech.[2] The Court had started limiting the use of patronage in the 1970s, as we shall see shortly, but had left open many issues including the degree to which hiring decisions could reflect politics. The issue now squarely presented was whether partisan ties could ever be used in public employment.

The coincidence of these two judgments on the same day provides an appropriate starting point for a closer look at politics and public service, the focus of this chapter. We should bear in mind the nexus between the two issues—the extent to which, on one hand, public employees are protected from patronage, while they are at the same time barred from taking an active part in political campaigns. The two issues are closely related. What is not always clear is how logical is that link, or how well the convergence of the two doctrines serves the needs and interests of the public service. We begin our analysis by revisiting the Hatch Act, then turn to patronage, and conclude with a brief review of the status of unions, strikes, and collective bargaining in the public service.

### Which public employees are covered by the Hatch Act?

[Note: At the time of publication, major revisions in the Hatch Act were under active consideration in Congress. The presence in the White House of a president who had promised to support such changes altered the prospects from the 1980s. In essence, the proposed revisions would allow federal officials to run for local (though not federal or state) office, and on their own time, and would permit federal employees to manage political campaigns and raise money for candiates in their off hours. But the Hatch Act would continue to forbid federal workers from using their positions or information they obtained through those positions for political ends. The House and Senate versions of the proposed changes differed materially, and many issues of both substance and process needed to be resolved before revision could take place.]

The Hatch Act[3] applies to most federal employees in the executive branch of the United States government, whether or not they are in the civil service. The law also applies to certain employees of state and local government whose major assignments are in departments funded in whole or part by federal appropriations. (As we will see shortly, the curbs on political activity have been substantially relaxed for state and local employees, though they are still generally covered by the Act.)

Persons employed by federally assisted educational or research institutions or by religious, cultural, or philanthropic organizations are not affected by the Hatch Act. Nor does it reach persons paid from appropriations for the Office of the President, the heads and assistant heads of executive departments, those appointed by the President with the advice and consent of the Senate who engage in major policy determinations, and certain administrators of the District of Columbia.

**What political activities are forbidden by the Hatch Act?**

The language of the Hatch Act makes it unlawful for an executive agency employee to use his official authority or influence for the purpose of interfering with or affecting the result of an election."[4] The law continues: "[No officer or employee covered by the Act shall] take any active part in political management or political campaigns."[5] Such language does not, of course, give any detailed guidance to government employees contemplating some role in politics. The Hatch Act in fact nowhere provides that sort of detailed guidance. Rather, what it does is to incorporate by reference more than 3,000 rulings that had issued by the United States Civil Service Commission between 1883 and the enactment of the law. These rulings had been codified at times by the commission, and later by the Merit Systems Protection Board, although the process of seeking guidance in this gray area of the law may be a daunting task for the conscientious public worker. One source of potential guidance is a "hot line" for inquiries about Hatch Act coverage, at (202) 653-7143.

The Hatch Act is concerned both with political pressure and coercion applied from above within the public service, and with wholly voluntary partisan activity of workers at all levels. Thus covered federal employees may not use their official authority to influence the outcome of an election, nor may they take any active part in the management or conduct of a political campaign. Specifically, they may not be candidates for, or hold office in, any national, state, or local partisan organization; leadership in such an organization is forbidden even if the particular role is remote from frontline politics but still might be considered a part of the overall management of the organization. A federal employee may not solicit funds, directly or indirectly, for partisan political purposes or organize or promote fund-raising for a political cause. Federal employees may not themselves be candidates of political parties for elected office; even passive consent to a campaign organized by friends might be considered a violation of the Act. Nor may a federal employee express personal endorsement of, or opposition to, a partisan candidate in a political advertisement. Circulating a nominating petition for a partisan candidate is also forbidden.

These are in summary form the broad constraints imposed

by the Hatch Act. Until 1974, the same rules applied to state and local employees on federally funded projects and programs. But in that year Congress exempted state and local workers from the restrictions on taking part in or directing political campaigns,[6] thus opening a substantial gap between the levels of government. A covered state or local worker is still forbidden to coerce or pressure a subordinate or co-worker for political purposes and may still not serve as a partisan candidate. But most other activities denied to federal employees seem to be open to those who are covered at the state and local level.

### What political activities does the Hatch Act specifically permit to covered workers?

The Act says only that an employee or individual covered by the Hatch Act restrictions "shall retain the right to vote as he chooses and to express his opinion on all political subjects and candidates"—though, as we have seen, that latter phrase does not include using one's name in an endorsement or opposition advertisement for or against a candidate. The scope of these rights has been only partially defined by the commission (later board) rulings and court decisions. But the following guidelines may be helpful:

A covered worker may register and may vote in a party primary as well as a general election without fear of reprisal. He or she may freely contribute money to any candidate or party (subject, of course, to the limits imposed on all citizens by the Federal Election Campaign Reform Act). Individual opinions on political issues and on candidates may be expressed both publicly and privately. Political posters, badges, buttons, and other insignia may be worn and displayed. Federal employees may belong to political organizations, so long as they do not assume a leadership role. They may attend political gatherings, provided they do not publicly display partisanship. A federal employee may even hold certain minor elected offices, such as justice of the peace, notary public, election judge, or commissioner, and may serve on local school boards or library boards and public governing boards for charitable and educational branches of state and local government.

Since the major concern of the Hatch Act is with partisan politics, there is greater latitude for nonpartisan activities. An election is deemed nonpartisan if none of the candidates represents a party for which a presidential elector received votes in the previous national election, regardless of whether opposing sides are taken on local issues. Under such conditions, a federal employee is permitted to seek a nonpartisan elective office, and is also allowed to take a more active role in a nonpartisan political organization than is allowable in a regular political party.

The activities permitted to state and local employees under the 1974 revision of the Hatch Act are substantially broader. Even those who work on federally funded projects may, for example, hold membership and may even hold office in political organizations; may run for office within political parties; may make speeches or solicit voters in support of, or opposition to, partisan candidates; may originate and sign nominating petitions for partisan candidates; may drive voters to the polls; and may (without coercion, of course) solicit contributions for partisan candidates or causes. (One important caution: As we shall see shortly, there may be state or local laws more restrictive than the modified Hatch Act and thus would supersede the Hatch rules for all covered state or local employee.)

**Do special rules apply to federal employees in communities where a majority of people work for the federal government?**

In these so-called federally impacted areas, the Office of Personnel Management has discretion to modify the Hatch Act restrictions.[7] Under those conditions, it may be possible for a federal worker to be an independent candidate for office even in a partisan election, and to support or oppose such independent candidates. Political activity must still not interfere with an employee's primary responsibility to the federal government and to the agency and must not serve to create a conflict of interest.

**How does the Hatch Act square with the constitutional rights of public employees?**

Clearly the Hatch Act limits the political activity of public workers far more extensively than would be constitutionally permissible for citizens at large. People who enter the federal service thus surrender important rights of citizenship as a condition of the jobs they seek. To return once more to Justice

Holmes's maxim, it is not clear that federal workers have a right to be policemen and freely to "talk politics."

A carefully planned challenge to the Hatch Act's constitutionality reached the Supreme Court very soon after the law went into effect. While most of the claims were rejected as premature because the plaintiffs had not yet done any of the political acts they feared might endanger their jobs, the Court did reach the merits in one of the cases and decisively sustained the substantial curtailment of public employees' political freedoms.[8] Quite simply, said the justices, Congress had acted to protect strong governmental interests that outweighed the political freedoms of the individual workers.[9]

The case before the Court was an especially appealing one for the constitutional claims. The employee was a roller in the Philadelphia mint—hardly a highly visible person whose politics would compromise the government. And his partisan activity had taken place on his own time, away from the job site, with no apparent affect on fellow workers. Yet the Court still deferred to the judgment of Congress that the only way to keep politics out of the federal service was to sweep with broad strokes: "Evidently what Congress feared was the cumulative effect on employee morale of political activity by all employees who could be induced to participate actively."[10] Such a concern was enough to outweigh the substantial First Amendment claims the workers had made. Moreover, the Court observed, the Act "leaves untouched full participation by employees in political decisions at the ballot box and forbids only the partisan activity of federal personnel deemed offensive to efficiency."[11]

There matters stood for two decades. By the 1970s, many observers felt change in the wind. The Supreme Court's view of limits on government benefits—and especially public employment—had changed dramatically. Meanwhile, the Civil Service Commission had done little to clarify the scope and reach of the Hatch Act; the only real basis for guidance remained those three thousand rulings that had been incorporated by reference into the Act, but had never been codified into formal rules or regulations. So a federal district judge revisited the issue and predicted that the Supreme Court would reverse itself if given the chance in a new case. He therefore struck down the Hatch Act partly because of the uncertainty of its key provisions, and partly because the law denied federal workers and their families a major role "in a society where political speech and uninhibited, robust, wide-open debate on public issues are at the essence of self-government."[12]

To the surprise of most close observers, the district judge turned out to be quite wrong in his prediction. A very different Supreme Court overwhelmingly reaffirmed its predecessors' view of the validity of the Hatch Act.[13] The justices again recognized "the judgment of history . . . that it is in the best interests of the country, indeed essential, that federal service should depend upon meritorious performance rather than political service, and that the political influence of federal employees and others on the electoral process should be limited."[14] Thus a Court that had boldly applied the doctrine of unconstitutional conditions to many types of government benefits, and most especially to public employment, stopped surprisingly short of the full implications of that doctrine for political activity in the public service. The countervailing interests that had impelled Congress in 1939 and had persuaded the Supreme Court in 1947 once again prevailed.

With the judicial door now firmly closed, attention moved back to Congress. Several national study groups urged some relaxation of restrictions that were not only vague and cumbersome but to many no longer seemed necessary or even appropriate in the 1980s. Proponents of Hatch Act reform argued that conditions in the federal service had changed markedly since 1939. Not only had public employee unions assumed a far stronger role in protecting employee rights. Moreover, the safeguards of procedural due process, virtually unknown when the Act was adopted, had expanded dramatically in the intervening years. Thus the federal worker who had once been almost helpless against political coercion or intimidation now enjoyed an impressive array of protections that reduced the need for resort to the Hatch Act.

Congress was more persuaded than had been the Supreme Court of the case for reform. Starting in the mid 1970s, various amendments received favorable legislative attention, followed by executive disapproval. The version that reached the President's desk in the summer of 1990 would still have forbidden federal workers from running for partisan elective office, engaging in political activity on the job, or soliciting direct political contributions. But it would have removed the major constraints on off-duty political activity—allowing federal workers to serve as campaign and party officials and to run as delegates to party conventions. It would also have allowed them to solicit contributions for the political action committees of the several federal and postal employee unions—a reform that was less universally acclaimed.

But President Bush (like Presidents Ford and Reagan before him) had promised to veto any such changes, and veto he did, arguing that "the obvious result of enactment would be unstated but enormous pressure to participate in partisan political activity."[15] Such risks were the greater, insisted the President, because "they arise in a climate in which the unspoken assumption is that political conformity is the route to achievement and security."[16] Efforts to override the veto succeeded in the House, but by two votes ultimately failed in the Senate—even though the Senate had earlier passed the reform by more than two thirds. Thus the saga ended, at least for now.

## How does a Hatch Act violation charge proceed?

The recent case of Augustine Narcisse offers a good example.[17] She was employed as a civilian typist for the United States Air Force at Lowrey Air Base near Denver. During the 1988 presidential campaign she worked part time evenings and weekends as a "volunteer" (at $4 an hour) on behalf of Governor Dukakis. She did some telephone polling during the weeks leading up to the election. On the evening of November 1, she was interviewed by a reporter for a Denver television station, which broadcast portions of the interview later that evening.

Soon thereafter, the Office of Special Counsel filed against Ms. Narcisse two charges of Hatch Act violation. The first count alleged that she had been employed as a paid volunteer for the Colorado Committee to Elect Michael Dukakis, a partisan organization. The other count alleged that she had publicly endorsed and solicited votes for Governor Dukakis during the television interview. The case was assigned to the chief administrative law judge of the Merit Systems Protection Board— the agency charged with enforcing and interpreting the Hatch Act—who then conducted a full hearing on the charges.

The administrative law judge ruled in Ms. Narcisse's favor on both counts—finding on the first count insufficient proof that she had actually worked for a partisan organization, or that she was being charged on the basis of her activities there (as opposed to merely working for a political committee, which was not a violation). On the second count, the administrative judge found that in the televised interview (which was quite impromptu) Narcisse had expressed only her personal opinion about a candidate—a permissible activity. He was also impressed by the fact the reporter had simply dropped in unannounced, a fact which dispelled any inference that Narcise sought a platform for her views.

The Special Counsel appealed the case to the Merit Systems Protection Board, which heard argument from both sides and sustained the administrative judge's ruling on both counts. But the board went beyond an analysis of the facts and added an important comment about the law that gives us valuable insight into the workings and interpretation of the Hatch Act: On the first count, "assuming that [Narcisse] was employed by a partisan campaign organization, her telephone polling did not constitute 'taking an active part in . . . political campaigns' within the meaning of [the Hatch Act]."[18] The basis for that ruling was not the board's own view of the Act but the absence of any pre-1940 ruling that made such activity unlawful, largely reflecting the recency of telephone polling as a possibly suspect practice.

Only by treating the scope of the Act as essentially openended could such activity be brought within its sanctions—and that was something the board was quite clear neither Congress nor the Supreme Court had intended. Thus the complaint was dismissed. Augustine Narcisse retained both her federal job and, to a limited degree, her right to "talk politics." The lessons of the case are that an accused federal employee does get her day in court, or at least before the board, and that any charges against her must not only fit the facts but must also fit within the activities Congress meant to forbid in adopting the Hatch Act.

### May states and localities limit the political activities of their employees apart from the Hatch Act?

Clearly they may, and many do. Some such laws are patterned largely after the Hatch Act, and in light of the two United States Supreme Court cases sustaining its provisions those laws would clearly survive a challenge under the United

States Constitution. State laws that differ from the Hatch Act but do not go substantially further are likely to be sustained on similar grounds. Thus in 1982 the Supreme Court held that Texas could, if it wished, bar certain elected state officials from seeking other elective office or even announcing candidacy during the term they currently served.[19] Texas also provided that if certain officials declared for any other federal or state elective office more than a year before the end of their current terms, they would be treated as having automatically resigned their present offices.

The Court recognized the potential severity of such a choice but sustained both Texas laws against challenges of several types. When it came to free speech claims, the justices felt Texas had imposed "a far more limited restriction on political activity than this Court has upheld with regard to civil servants,"[20] citing the two Hatch Act cases. Whatever burden Texas law imposed was "insignificant" by comparison, and that was the end of the matter.

While the United States Constitution may not avail here, states are free to interpret their own constitutions in ways that give their citizens, including public employees, greater freedoms than the Bill of Rights ensures. Thus the California Supreme Court some years ago announced a rigorous constitutional standard that must be followed in judging state or local laws affecting government workers: "A government agency which would require a waiver of constitutional rights as a condition of public employment must demonstrate (1) that the political restraints rationally relate to the enhancement of the public service; (2) that the benefits outweigh the resulting impairment of constitutional rights, and (3) that no alternatives less subversive of constitutional rights are available."[21]

Under that test, the California court held that a county hospital nurse had a constitutional right to distribute literature and circulate petitions in a campaign to recall the hospital district board—activities for which she had been fired. The ban that triggered her dismissal seemed to the court to sweep far too broadly and was quite likely to chill protected activity and expression. But there was a basic premise in the California opinion that offers a fascinating contrast to the U.S. Supreme Court's view of these issues:

As the number of persons employed by government and governmentally assisted institutions continue to grow, the necessity of preserving for them the maximum practicable right to participate in the political life of the republic grows with it. Restrictions on public employees which, in some or all of their applications, advance no compelling public interest commensurate with the waiver of constitutional rights which they require, imperil the continued operation of our institutions of representative government.[22]

### May state and local employees be barred from running for office?

The 1982 Supreme Court case we just noted literally upheld only a deferral or postponement of the right to seek other elective office. The dissenters, however, argued that the judgment effectively "bars the candidacy of a wide range of state, federal and foreign office holders."[23] Moreover, the Court stressed that the restrictions affected only elected officials, who could be said to have accepted greater burdens than the general run of appointed public workers. Nonetheless, the majority's approach would go far to sustain state and local limits on public employees' running for, or declaring an intent to run for, elective offices.

Some lower courts have taken a more protective view in cases that are factually distinguishable. The California and Oregon supreme courts years ago held that state laws barring the seeking of elective office abridged free speech more than was necessary to prevent actual conflicts of interest or disruption of the public service.[24] Several years later a federal appeals court reached a similar conclusion with regard to a Cranston, Rhode Island, city charter provision that required the dismissal of any municipal employee who became a candidate for nomination or election to public office.[25] The court noted that declaring candidacy for office was an especially strong form of expression, and one for which public employees were well suited.

Thus any law that restricted candidacy must be reviewed with special care, since it affected a "fundamental" human right. The court recognized that a city had a valid interest in "maintaining the honesty and impartiality of its public work force"[26] but concluded that this interest could be served by asking officials to take leaves of absence to campaign. The city's interests could also be served by narrower restrictions, such as those reaching only employees "whose positions make them vulnerable to corruption and conflict of interest."[27] If particular abuses of office were shown during a campaign, the city could then punish the offender directly.

These cases indicate important exceptions to any general rules about the rights of public employees to run for office:

First, requiring that such persons take a leave of absence seems quite reasonable, and several courts have so held.

Second, there may be sensitive situations in which simply running for office may undermine a close relationship of trust and thus warrant dismissal—as a federal appeals court found in the case of a deputy city attorney,[28] and another federal appellate court held in regard to personnel of a particularly sensitive and visible agency.[29]

Third, government clearly has an interest in checking campaigns that divert time, energy and commitment substantially away from the employee's primary tasks.

Finally, the employee who runs against a superior within the same agency poses a special risk. Even the California Supreme Court, which has been as protective as any of public workers' political rights, conceded that "a strong case . . . can be made that a public employee's decision to . . . run or campaign against his own superior has so disruptive an effect on the public service as to warrant prohibition." While the nature of the relationship may bear scrutiny, since not all subordinates pose such a threat to anyone up the line, the interest in limiting candidacy here is an unusually strong one and has been so recognized.[30]

### May a person be discharged from a government job for political reasons?

For most positions, the answer is no. Party affiliation had been used throughout American history as a basis for hiring and firing in the public sector. When parties changed, one of the first things a new administration would do was to fire those who belonged to the "wrong" party and were not protected by civil service systems—roughly half of all public employees. Or they might be given the option of keeping their jobs by changing parties. This practice of patronage dismissal was quite common, and accepted simply as a fact of political life, until very recently.

Constitutional challenges to patronage dismissal were taken to court in the 1970s. The issue reached the Supreme Court in 1976, in the case of *Elrod v. Burns*,[31] which for the first time gave First Amendment protection to the vast number of public workers who were not covered by civil service and thus might lose their jobs if their party lost power, or even if they refused to support the party that was in power.

The Court in *Elrod* held that a patronage dismissal was, quite simply, an abridgment of free expression; the choice it forced the public employee to make was "tantamount to coerced belief."[32] Not only was it financial support that created the problem, "even a pledge of allegiance to another party . . . only serves to compromise the individual's true beliefs."[33] If a person could not be denied a government job for belonging to the Communist party or the Ku Klux Klan, as the Court had earlier made clear, then membership in the Republican or Democratic party (or refusal to join either party) hardly seemed a valid reason for firing an otherwise qualified employee.

Nor could such a burden be justified by the interests government advanced in its support; promoting efficiency in, and loyalty to, government through party incentives, creating continuity and commitment—these and other asserted benefits either could not be shown at all or, to the extent they did exist, were not strong enough to offset the harm patronage did to the individual's beliefs and associations. In fact, the majority identified ways in which it believed patronage dismissal actually hindered, rather than helped, just those interests that had been asserted by the government agencies seeking to defend patronage practices.

Beyond the effect on the individual, the *Elrod* Court was also deeply troubled by what it felt patronage dismissal did to the entire public service:

> Conditioning public employment on partisan support prevents support of competing political interests. Existing employees are deterred from such support, as well as the multitude seeking jobs. As government employment, state or federal, becomes more pervasive, the greater the dependence on it becomes, and therefore the greater be-

comes the power to starve political opposition by commanding partisan support, financial or otherwise. Patronage thus tips the electoral process in favor of the incumbent party, and where the practice's scope is substantial relative to the size of the electorate, the impact on the process can be significant.[34]

## May party affiliation be used by government employers in other ways—for promotion, transfer, recall after layoff, or initial hiring?

The *Elrod* case dealt only with patronage dismissal. For some years thereafter, the legality of other uses of patronage remained in doubt, though government agencies continued to apply political tests to almost everything but dismissal. As late as 1989, the federal appeals court from which the *Elrod* case had come refused to extend that doctrine beyond its facts and thus upheld other use of patronage and politics. But the Supreme Court was ready by the summer of 1990 to go the one critical step further, and in *Rutan v. Republican Party of Illinois*[35] held that all uses of patronage—for most employees— was inconsistent with public workers' First Amendment rights.

Despite an impassioned dissent, the majority felt the issue had really been resolved by *Elrod*: "It is unnecessary here to consider whether not being hired is less burdensome than being discharged because the government is not pressed to do either on the basis of political affiliation. The question in the patronage context is not which penalty is more acute but whether the government, without sufficient justification, is pressuring employees to discontinue the free exercise of their First Amendment rights."[36] Thus the use of politics to transfer a person or to refuse to hire, recall, or promote was constitutionally indistinguishable from the long-barred use of patronage for discharge or dismissal purposes.

## Do all public employees enjoy the same extent of protection against patronage actions?

No, for there is one key exception to the *Elrod-Rutan* doctrine. In the initial case the Supreme Court left open the possibility that patronage might be used in certain policymaking positions if party loyalty could be shown to be crucial to the position. The Court did not at that time define the scope of the exception, recognizing that no clear line could easily be drawn. The key, said the justices, was the "nature of the responsibilities" rather than the place in the structure or organization.

The Court then revisited the exception and its scope in *Branti v. Finkel*[37] four years later. After reaffirming Elrod's basic principle, the Court sought to define more clearly what employees were still subject to patronage actions. "If," said the Branti majority, "an employee's private political beliefs would interfere with the discharge of his public duties, his First Amendment rights may be required to yield to the State's vital interest in maintaining governmental effectiveness and efficiency."[38] "Policymaking" no longer looked like the sole or even primary test. On one hand, "party affiliation is not necessarily relevant to every policymaking or confidential position."[39]

On the other hand, party loyalty might reasonably be expected in some nonpolicy staff positions; a Governor may insist that the duties of certain key aides and assistants "cannot be performed effectively unless those persons share his political beliefs and party commitments."[40] Thus the ultimate inquiry should not be whether the position is one that makes policy or is inherently confidential, but whether "the hiring authority can demonstrate that party affiliation is an appropriate requirement for the effective performance of the public office involved."[41]

Cases at both ends of this spectrum may be relatively easy—high-ranking policymaking executive staff members of the Indiana State Department of Education on one end[42] and an Illinois state capitol custodian at the other end.[43] In between there are many difficult, not yet fully resolved, questions that can only be addressed on a case-by-case basis with the best guidance that the *Elrod-Branti-Rutan* principles and the underlying logic will provide. Perhaps the only other point that is clear is an important one of procedure: government always bears the burden of proving that a particular position so clearly demands party loyalty or compatibility that it falls outside the *Elrod* zone of protection. The employee receives the full benefit of any doubt on that issue.

**What political affiliation rights does an unprotected employee retain?**

While an employee who cannot claim *Elrod* and *Rutan* protection may to a far greater degree be at the mercy of politics, some residual interests remain. Surely such a person could not be required to sign a partisan loyalty oath of a kind that would violate the public worker's general freedoms. Nor could such a person be forced to express publicly an abhorrent view or publicly endorse an uncongenial candidate or vote against conscience. At least a modicum of personal freedom remains, even for one whose position and responsibilities make him or her in some degree a prisoner of politics.

**May an adverse personnel action for which no reason is given be challenged on patronage grounds?**

Such a challenge would of course be much more difficult than in the case where the action clearly and unequivocally reflects partisan politics. Yet there may still be ways in which to establish such a motive—if, for example, all the people who were fired or not hired by a given administration are of the "wrong" party, while all those who were favored are partisans of that administration, a political motive could probably be inferred.

That process might also depend substantially on the stated grounds for denying or terminating employment; if the grounds are clearly limited by statute, an unexplained adverse action in a politically volatile atmosphere might well support such an inference.

**Do the patronage hiring and dismissal cases affect persons in the civil service?**

Not directly, since the reason for creating the civil service in the first place was to make merit and ability, rather than party, the basis for hiring and promoting a substantial part of the public workforce. It is unlikely that a civil servant would be subject to patronage action, given the likelihood that any such action would be set aside. And if such action were taken, only if the civil service protections failed would there be any need to seek constitutional protection.

**Does a public employee have a right to join a labor union?**

Yes, even if that union advocates strikes in a jurisdiction where strikes are unlawful. A federal court of appeals held that teachers had been unconstitutionally dismissed for having been members of a labor union.[44] Such affiliation, said the court, was within the teachers' freedom of association. Even if the union actually engaged in illegal activity, such as a strike, the members could not be penalized as a group for that reason. Similarly, another court held that Washington, D.C., police officers could not be barred from joining a union because it advocated illegal strikes: "Clearly, this sweeping restriction on a policeman's right to join others in advocating protected ideas cannot stand."[45] Governmental concern about unlawful strikes must be addressed through "precise legislation to protect the public."

Courts have expanded such protection beyond mere union membership. Public employees may assume leadership roles in such organizations, may recruit new members, may represent the union in dealing with the public and with the employer. A teacher, one court has said, "may not be denied a teaching contract because of his actions in a professional association, regardless of how vigorous they are."[46]

**Can a public employee insist that union dues be withheld from his paycheck?**

No. In a 1976 case, the Supreme Court sustained a city's refusal to withhold union dues as part of a general checkoff system for employee contributions to charities and other public causes to which all might contribute.[47] In a right-to-work state where public employee collective bargaining was unlawful, the city was justified in barring union dues from the checkoff list. The city workers' undoubted right to join the union did not extend as far as to require the city to collect their dues and turn those dues over to the union.

**Can supervisors and administrators be barred from joining the same union to which rank-and-file employees belong?**

The public sector labor laws of some states do require separation of supervisors and workers, and courts have generally sustained such rules in the interest of avoiding conflicts of interest and in maintaining discipline within certain employment sectors. But there is at least one judgment to the contrary. Some years ago a federal court in Florida struck down a law that barred administrators and supervisors from belonging to the same union that represented regular classroom teachers.[48]

## Do public employees have a right to bargain collectively?

Only if statutes permit them to do so. Civilian federal employees are permitted, under Executive Order 11,491, a limited scope of bargaining. The National Labor Relations Board, which authorizes and regulates private sector bargaining, has no jurisdiction over government employees. Many states authorize public sector bargaining through state labor boards. But where such authorization is absent, courts seldom insist that public employers bargain. One court responded in this way to a constitutional claim: "There is no question that the right of public employees to associate for the purpose of collective bargaining is a right protected by the First and Fourteenth Amendments to the Constitution. But there is no constitutional duty to bargain collectively with an exclusive bargaining agent. Such duty, when imposed, is imposed by statute."[49]

## May government bargain with some but not all public employees?

In general, selective bargaining has been allowed by the courts if the distinction serves a rational end. Two federal courts sustained such partial bargaining arrangements—in both cases extending bargaining to the general run of employees but denying it to police officers.[50] Such cases seem to recognize and accept a governmental policy to treat law enforcement differently. A similar rationale for separation and partial bargaining may also apply in other sectors—especially where professional specialties or occupational interests would justify disparate treatment of employee subgroups within an employment setting or workplace.

## Do public employees have a right to picket peacefully against agency policy?

Within certain limits, they do. To some degree the answer may turn on the *Pickering* case, which we discussed in chapter III. Otherwise, courts recognize that picketing is a well-established form of expression, designed to convey political and other messages. Such judgments caution, though, that mass picketing and picketing that blocks or obstructs the passage of others may exceed the First Amendment protection and thus be curtailed. Courts have also shown a willingness to enjoin public employee picketing that advocates an unlawful strike or work stoppage.

### Do public employees have a right to strike?

Not as a matter of federal constitutional law. One federal court recently observed: "It seems clear that public employees stand on no stronger footing in this regard than private employers and that in the absence of a statute, they too do not possess the right to strike."[51] The scope of federal authority in this area was tested during the strike in the early 1980s by the Professional Air Traffic Controllers Organization and the systematic replacement by the Reagan administration of strikers who refused to return following a court order.

State law may vary substantially. Some states confer a right to strike on their employees. Apart from statutory authority, state courts may find a basis for a right to strike elsewhere—for example, the California Supreme Court's judgment that public workers have a common-law right to engage in strikes that do not create a substantial or imminent threat to public health or safety. In California the legislature left the issue to the courts. It forbade only firefighters to strike; as to other public employees, strikes were neither forbidden nor allowed. Apart from the common-law basis for permitting nonessential public employee strikes, the California court found a certain symmetry: "[Society] tolerate[s] strikes by private employees in many of the same areas in which government is engaged, such as transportation, health, education, and utilities."[52]

Thus the short answer is that public employees strike at their peril in the absence of clear authority—from a court or a legislature—for doing so. The constitutional rights to join unions and to picket peacefully have never been held to include striking. Moreover, the risks of a wrong choice may be severe. The penalty for engaging in an illegal strike is often immediate discharge or dismissal, and courts which recognize that government can bar strikes tend also to sustain such severe reprisals.

**Can a public employee refuse to join or support a union?**

While it seems clear that a public employee may not be forced against his or her will to become a regular member of a union, the question of support through union dues is far less clear. In 1977 the Supreme Court held that public workers could be required to pay dues to support a union that had been recognized as the bargaining agent for a unit in which they were employed.[53] Requiring all to pay seemed a reasonable accommodation, and the only feasible way to avoid a possible exit for many union members who simply wished the benefits of representation without any obligation to pay. The Court recognized, however, that those who objected to certain activities of the union were entitled to some proration of the dues, reflecting the core activities of the union.

The later cases on this issue became increasingly complex and technical, culminating in a 1991 Supreme Court judgment that sustained most of the provisions and procedures of Michigan's public employee laws[54] (also the focus of the 1977 case). Through these cases the Court has established standards by which to judge what portion of the dues a dissenting unit member may be required to pay: chargeable activities must (1) be germane to collective bargaining activity; (2) be justified by the government's undoubted interest in labor peace and in avoiding "free riders" who benefit from union efforts without having to pay; and (3) must not add significantly to the burdening of free speech that is inherent in the allowance of an agency or union shop.

The process for determining the amount of the fee that may be charged to all unit members has become exceedingly complex. Courts scrutinize specific activities, programs, and even publications of a public employee union to determine which ones meet the test and which do not. Thus, for example, under the 1991 case on the Michigan law, faculty members at a state university may be charged a pro rata share of the costs of collective-bargaining activities of state and national affiliates that are not directly related to the bargaining unit, and for portions of union publications that generally concern teaching and education, including professional development. But they may not be charged for union programs that are designed generally to secure funds for support of public education, or for the general costs of union public relations efforts that are not directly related to collective bargaining activity.

### In what other ways may public sector bargaining affect the employee's freedom of expression?

One case clearly defines that relationship and sets important limits on the inevitable tension between bargaining and free speech. During a Madison, Wisconsin, school board meeting, the union that represented the teachers objected to a statement from a nonunion teacher about a clause in the agreement that was then being negotiated. The teacher read a petition, signed by some fellow teachers, all of whom objected to the challenged contract provision. The union then claimed the school board had committed an unfair labor practice by allowing a teacher to address the board directly. The state employment relations commission agreed, holding that teachers could be denied the right to speak, even at public meetings, "on matters subject to collective bargaining."[55] The Wisconsin Supreme Court affirmed, finding that an individual teacher's petition to the school board posed a "clear and present danger."[56]

The United States Supreme Court reversed and ruled unanimously in favor of the teacher and the board.[57] Since the board meeting was a public session, and since the teacher was not seeking to negotiate for himself or anyone else—that might have been a quite different issue—the board could not limit a citizen's freedom of speech because of his occupation or union membership (or nonmembership), or because of the views he sought to express. Apart from the individual teacher's free speech rights, there was a larger interest of public policy: "Restraining teachers' expressions to the board on matters involving the operation of the schools would seriously impair the board's ability to govern the district."[58]

This statement from the unanimous Supreme Court judgment is surely reminiscent of similar reasoning in the *Pickering* case, and suggests a recurrent theme. Protecting the free expression of public employees is of course vital to the interests of individual employees and to the community of public workers. But there are even larger societal and governmental interests that call for broad latitude in defining employees rights. Those interests are equally present when, as in the Madison case, the agency wishes to hear what the employee has to say, and in cases like *Pickering*, where the agency—or at least the agency head—wishes to silence the speaker. Tolerance for the public employee's message is equally essential in both situations.

## NOTES

1. Washington Post, June 22, 1990, at p. A1, col. 6.
2. *Rutan v. Republican Party of Illinois*, 497 U.S. 62 (1991).
3. 5 U.S.C. § 7324 (1988).
4. 5 U.S.C. § 7324(a)(1) (1988).
5. 5 U.S.C. § 7324(b) (1988).
6. Public L. No. 93–443, § 401(b)(1), §§ 1501–1503, 88 Stat. 1290 (1974) (codified as amended 5 U.S.C. §§ 1501–1502 (1988)).
7. 5 U.S.C. § 7327(b) (1988); 5 C.F.R. 733.124; *see Democratic State Central Committee of Montgomery County v. Andolsek*, 249 F. Supp. 1009 (D. Md. 1966).
8. *United Public Workers v. Mitchell*, 330 U.S. 75 (1947).
9. 330 U.S. at 102–4.
10. 330 U.S. at 102–3.
11. 330 U.S. at 101.
12. *National Association of Letter Carriers v. United States Civil Service Commission*, 346 F. Supp. 578 (D.D.C. 1972).
13. *United States Civil Service Commission v. National Association of Letter Carriers*, 413 U.S. 547 (1973).
14. 413 U.S. at 579.
15. Washington Post, June 16, 1992, at. A1, cols. 5–6.
16. *Id.*
17. *Special Counsel v. Narcisse*, Docket No. HQ12169010013, Merit Systems Protection Board, Nov. 20, 1991.
18. *Id.* at 8–9.
19. *Clements v. Fashing*, 457 U.S. 957 (1982).
20. 457 U.S. at 972.
21. *Bagley v. Washington Township Hospital District*, 65 Cal. 2d 499, 501–2, 421 P.2d 409, 411, 55 Cal. Rptr. 401, 403 (1966).
22. 65 Cal. 2d at 510–11, 421 P.2d at 417, 55 Cal. Rptr. at 409.
23. *Clements v. Fashing*, 457 U.S. 957, 987 (1982) (dissenting opinion).
24. *Fort v. Civil Service Commission*, 61 Cal. 2d 331, 392 P.2d 385, 38 Cal. Rptr. 625 (1965); *Minielly v. State*, 242 Ore. 490, 411 P.2d 69 (1966).

25. *Mancuso v. Taft*, 476 F.2d 187 (1st Cir. 1973).
26. *Id.* at 198.
27. *Ibid.*
28. *Ibid.*
29. *Newcomb v. Brannan*, 558 F.2d 825 (7th Cir. 1977).
30. *Fort v. Civil Service Commission*, 61 Cal. 2d 331, 338, 38 Cal. Rptr. 625, 629, 392 P.2d 385, 389 (1964).
31. 427 U.S. 347 (1976).
32. 427 U.S. at 355.
33. 427 U.S. at 356.
34. 427 U.S. at 151–52.
35. 111 L. Ed. 2d 52 (1991).
36. *Id.* at 69.
37. 445 U.S. 507 (1980).
38. *Id.* at 517.
39. *Id.* at 518.
40. *Id.*
41. *Id.*
42. *Indiana State Employees Association v. Negley*, 365 F. Supp. 225 (S.D. Ind. 1973).
43. *Illinois State Employees Association v. Lewis*, 473 F.2d 561 (7th Cir. 1972).
44. *McLauhglin v. Tilendis*, 398 F.2d 287 (7th Cir. 1968); *American Federation of State, County and Municipal Employees v. Woodward*, 406 F.2d 137 (8th Cir. 1969).
45. *Police Officers Guild, National Association of Police Officers v. Washington*, 369 F. Supp. 543, 552 D.D.C. 1973).
46. *Lee v. Smith*, GERR No. 383, B–15, B–16 (E.D. Va. 1971).
47. *City of Charlotte v. Firefighters, Local 660*, 426 U.S. 283 (1976).
48. *Orr v. Thorp*, 308 F. Supp. 1369 (S.D. Fla. 1969).
49. *Indianpolis Education Assocation v. Lewallen*, 72 LRRM 2071, 2072 (7th Cir. 1969).
50. *Confederation of Police v. City of Chicago*, 529 F.2d 89 (7th Cir. 1976); *Vorbeck v. McNeal*, 407 F. Supp. 733 (E.D. Mo. 1976).
51. *United Federation of Postal Clerks v. Blount*, 325 F. Supp. 879, 883 (D.D.C. 1971).
52. *County Sanitation District No. 2 of Los Angeles v. County Employees Association*, 38 Cal. 3d 564, 699 P.2d 835, 214 Cal. Rptr. 424 (1985).
53. *Abood v. Detroit Board of Education*, 431 U.S. 209 (1977).
54. *Lehnert v. Ferris Faculty Association*, 111 S. Ct. 1950 (1991).
55. *City of Madison, Joint School District No. 8 v. Wisconsin Employment Relations Commission*, 429 U.S. 167 (1976).

56.  *City of Madison, Joint School District No. 8 v. Wisconsin Employment Relations Board*, 231 N.W.2d 206, 208 (Wis. 1975).

57.  *Id.* at 212.

58.  429 U.S. at 177. *See also Princeton Education Association v. Princeton City School District*, 480 F. Supp. 962 (S.D. Ohio 1979).

# V

# The Private Lives of Public Employees

The scope of personal privacy remains, as it has long been, a major concern for those entering the public workforce Some issues are perennial—questions people would rather not answer about their finances, policies that inhibit associations and sexual activities off the job, adverse treatment of gay and lesbian employees, and physical searches of lockers, desks, and personal effects on the job. But the striking feature of public employee privacy is the emergence in the last decade of a whole new set of issues—drug testing of applicants and employees, testing for AIDS in the public workforce, checking public workers' cholesterol levels, and restrictions on such seemingly private activity as smoking at home on evenings and weekends.

Some of these new questions have been at least partially resolved. The Supreme Court has, for example, decided one major case on public employee drug testing[1]—though many would say the judgment opened more questions than it answered. But others of the new areas of controversy—AIDS testing being a prime example—are just beginning to get attention from the courts[2] and will probably be some time in process. Meanwhile, public workers who need and seek guidance may have simply to wait until these issues have been further clarified by courts and agencies. The goal of this chapter is to provide such guidance as the current state of the law permits.

### Does a public employee enjoy personal privacy at the work place?

The answer depends on a number of factors. After a series of inconclusive lower court cases, the Supreme Court addressed this issue in 1987. The case concerned Dr. Magno Ortega, a California state hospital psychiatrist, who brought suit against his superior after a search of his desk yielded damaging evidence used against him in a disciplinary proceeding. The justices eventually remanded the case to the trial court[3] and thus did not fully define the scope of an employee's constitutional zone of privacy, but along the way announced principles that offer at least partial guidance.

The Court first recognized that searches of public employees and of their effects at the workplace must be judged by Fourth Amendment standards. The next task was to delineate the "boundaries of the work-place context"[4] as a basis for gauging the scope of an employee's "expectation of privacy."[5] Thus a worker might reasonably have higher expectations about "a piece of closed personal luggage, a handbag or briefcase that happens to be within the employer's business address"[6] than would be the case for a desk or locker. Yet even as to the latter, public workers enjoyed a "reasonable expectation of privacy"; "individuals do not lose Fourth Amendment rights simply because they work for the government instead of a private employer."[7]

Judging how much privacy might "reasonably" be expected became the critical issue—one that must now be decided on a "case by case basis."[8] At one end were the suitcase and the briefcase that simply happened to be at the work site; at the other end, "some government offices may be so open to fellow employees or the public that no expectation of privacy is reasonable."[9] Dr. Ortega's situation fell somewhere along that spectrum; the circumstances showed that he did enjoy a reasonable expectation of privacy in the contents of his desk and file cabinets.

The scope of that expectation required the Court to "balance the invasion of the employee's legitimate expectations of privacy against the government's need for supervision, control, and the efficient operation of the work-place."[10] That balance would resolve the ultimate Fourth Amendment question—whether an agency or supervisor needed to obtain a search warrant before conducting a search. In general, deference to these substantial interests led the Court to dispense with such a need: "requiring an employer to obtain a warrant whenever the employer wished to enter an employee's office, desk or file cabinets for work-related purposes would seriously disrupt the routine conduct of business and would be unduly burdensome."[11]

Yet the analysis did not end quite there. Before validating a particular search, the Court insisted the agency action must be both "justified at its inception"[12] and "permissible in its scope."[13] Normally, a search would be "justified at its inception when there are reasonable grounds for suspecting that the search will turn up evidence that the employee is guilty of work-related misconduct or that the search is necessary for a noninvestigatory work-related purpose."[14] Under the second test the search would be "permissible in scope" when the means used are reasonably related to the object of the search and are not excessively intrusive with regard to the suspected misconduct.[15] It was these issues the justices sent back to the trial court, since they found any final delineation of Dr. Ortega's privacy claims to be premature.

Since the *Ortega* case, the lower courts have begun the complex process of applying its principles. On one hand, a federal court of appeals upheld a requirement that federal postal workers sign waivers warning that their lockers might be periodically searched by agency officials.[16] Since the basis for such random searches was the agency's reasonable suspicion of possession of drugs and weapons at the work place, the court held, under *Ortega*, that the workers had no reasonable expectation of privacy that would protect them from signing such waivers and facing the consequences. In a similar vein, a federal district court rejected privacy claims of Chicago firefighters who had objected to unannounced, warrantless searches of their lockers.[17] Here the reasonable expectation of privacy had been diminished by two factors this court found compelling— the pervasive extent of regulation of the field in which they worked, and department regulations that clearly put firefighters on notice that lockers were subject to warrantless searches to discover violations of strong department policies against possession of drugs or alcohol at the workplace.

On the other hand, a Florida appeals court ruled against a search of a state employee's desk on facts strikingly like those in *Ortega*.[18] Here the court found the circumstances insufficient to reduce the expectation of privacy that *Ortega* had recognized. The applicable agency regulations required "reasonable cause" for a warrantless search. "Cause" must be determined by the person with ultimate authority over the facility. The rules also gave the person with control over the area a chance initially to consent to the search. Those factors left the Florida court without the basis that *Ortega* required for finding the employee's expectation of workplace privacy to have been diminished.

It may still be too early to define fully the scope of *Ortega*.

Clearly the case marks a somewhat pyrrhic victory for public employee concerns about job-site privacy. The Court did recognize certain important protective principles and in one sense created a presumption of privacy in personal effects. Yet the case also established a ready basis for diluting or relaxing that protection and conducting warrantless, even random, searches under certain conditions. The zone of privacy seems clearly diminished where the agency can show a strong policy behind its intrusive practice—for example, the need to keep the work place free of drugs, alcohol or weapons—and can further demonstrate that only warrantless searches of desks and lockers will meet that need. As the federal postal workers, the Chicago firefighters, and others with post-*Ortega* challenges have discovered, courts are likely to give quite substantial deference to a government agency's claim of need to search for contraband without warning, at least in regard to such spaces as lockers and perhaps desks. It then becomes the employee's burden—and a substantial one—to show that the search was invalid in its inception or excessive in its scope.

### May an applicant or employee be required to answer questions about private conduct, activities, associations and the like?

In general, yes, although with some important qualifications. Courts have recognized that government as employer has a valid interest in knowing a good deal about those it hires. That interest will often include a range of past activities and associations—though, as we saw in chapter III, some inquiries into political belief and activity may violate First Amendment freedoms of expression. Otherwise, even when the agency might not be able to bar an applicant for giving the "wrong" answer, courts tend to resolve doubts in the agency's favor on a "there's no harm in asking" basis. One recent case illustrates that deference. The Philadelphia Police Department devised a questionnaire to aid in screening applicants for its newly created Special Investigative Unit, which would have responsibility for vice, discipline, and probing internal corruption. The questions covered a wide range of personal data such as criminal records of family members as well as the officer; extensive medical history including use and amount of prescription drugs, loans or debts in excess of $1,000 and other detailed financial data (e.g., gambling activity); and gifts and honoraria received by the applicant and family members. The department assured officers that any adverse information would not be used to jeopardize their police careers, and that an applicant for the Special Investigative Unit could withdraw without risk at any time. Yet some officers objected to the questionnaire, and their union took the matter to court.

A district judge held that such inquiries violated the officers' Fifth Amendment rights and enjoined the use of the questionnaire. But the court of appeals reversed.[19] With the possible exception of one question—asking about offices that family members held in profit or nonprofit entities—the court rejected the union's constitutional challenge to the questionnaire. Given the way it worked, the court found the application process "was not coercive." It entailed no risk for the officer who declined to apply in the first place or who, having started the process, later chose to withdraw. Even an officer who had been a member of the predecessor division to the Special Investigative Unit could freely opt out and would end up with a lateral transfer. Thus the only risk was that of a perjury charge for giving false information on the questionnaire—and that, the court noted, was a risk against which the Fifth Amendment gave public employees no greater protection than it gave any other citizens.

Another recent case casts a quite different light on this issue. In the spring of 1992 a federal district court barred the Defense Department from asking certain questions as the basis for issuing or renewing security clearances for civilian employees.[20] The questions asked about any and all arrests (including those for which the charges had been dismissed or the record expunged), financial status (specifically delinquent debt, bankruptcy filing, or tax liens), political party affiliation, and any past or present drug use or treatment for mental or psychological problems.

Such questions, ruled the judge, went beyond the Pentagon's valid needs in determining the security and loyalty of present or potential employees. The Defense Department, rather than appealing the decision, simply abandoned the invalid questions in order to prevent "disruption to the security program."

There are, however, important limits on the extent to which agencies can probe the private lives of their employees or applicants. For one, there must be a rational relationship between the question and a recognized interest of government as employer. Some years ago a federal appeals court held that agencies may not conduct a mere "fishing expedition" into an applicant's private life: "Only information which is reasonably necessary to make a determination" about the applicant's fitness may be sought. Another court observed that "governmental inquiries must be reasonably calculated to elicit information concerning an applicant's private . . . life which bears directly on his suitability for federal employment."[21]

Second, there must be some particular basis for asking about the area of private conduct in question. An agency would be hard put to justify, for example, asking every applicant in detail about his or her sexual activity, though such questions must be permissible in a few cases of special relevance or bearing to the person and the position. But not every applicant can be asked to disclaim or dispel adverse inferences for which no plausible basis exists.

Third, the cases make clear that a public worker's constitutional privacy interest may go well beyond simply political activities and associations. One court has noted that the First Amendment contains "a right . . . for an individual to keep private the details of his sex life."[22]

Fourth, the way in which the government interest is expressed is always relevant. Courts have noted the importance of "the clarity and rationality of the policies sought to be effectuated by the questions." One court added: "Where disclosure is required of circumstances of an intensely personal nature, the discloser is arguably entitled to know the standards by which his revelations will be assessed."[23]

Finally, the nature and sensitivity of the position surely affects the permissible scope of inquiry. As the *Philadelphia Police* case suggests, questions that might appropriately be asked of applicants for highly demanding or stressful roles would simply not be acceptable in hiring for a routine clerical or custodial position. One court has held, for example, that an applicant for a United States State Department post who admitted to having consulted a psychiatrist for "anxiety" could then be asked other probing questions about his sex life and drug use—questions that would not have been acceptable as routine initial inquiries. The partial disclosure, said the court, "furnished a reasonable basis for the agency to explore further the emotional stability [of an applicant] for the sensitive position involved."[24]

## What statutory protection of privacy do federal employees and applicants for federal jobs enjoy?

The Privacy Act of 1974[25] has given federal workers and those who seek federal positions substantial protection. This law requires most federal agencies to tell every individual from whom personal information is sought several things: (1) the legal authority on which the request is based; (2) the principal purpose for which the information is intended to be used; (3) the routine uses that may be made of the information (including those who may have access to it); and (4) the effect, if any, on the applicant's chances of refusing to provide any or all of the requested information. Agencies are even required to provide similar disclosures in asking for social security numbers; an individual must be told whether the response is mandatory or optional, and what use will be made of the number if it is given.

The Privacy Act permits a person who believes the notice requirements have not been observed to sue the agency in a federal court. Damages may be awarded if the court finds that the agency intentionally or willfully misrepresented the reasons for, or the intended use of, the information it sought.[26] Many state laws confer comparable protection on applicants for state and local employment, though provisions and the scope of protection, as well as procedures and remedies, vary widely.

## May an applicant or employee be required to disclose personal financial data?

For the most part, such requests have been upheld. The *Philadelphia Police* case allowed sweeping requests for financial data, not only about the applicant, but about family members as well—debts, loans, property holdings, honoraria and the like.[27] Such inquiries have generally been sustained, especially in the aftermath of Watergate and other scandals that heightened national concern about integrity and possible conflicts of interest in the public service. A rare exception is a California Supreme Court decision that struck down such a disclosure requirement because it was not limited to assets and holdings that posed a risk of conflict of interest.[28] But since that time many other courts have upheld such requirements, and the

Supreme Court has refused to review these judgments.[29] The laws that have been sustained generally concern positions to which integrity and trust are important; there have been few attempts to probe the finances of custodians and laborers, and the fate of such inquiries in the courts remains a matter of conjecture.

### May an applicant or employee be asked about past criminal activity?

In general, yes. At least where the questions are "specifically, directly and narrowly related to the performance of his official duties," the employee may be compelled to respond.[30] There is one important limitation, suggested again by the *Philadelphia Police* case: the Supreme Court has held that a public employee may not be fired solely for invoking the privilege against self-incrimination when faced with such an inquiry.[31] Nor may a person be dismissed for refusing to waive immunity from prosecution in return for testifying.[32] Thus there is a clear obligation to respond, which the applicant cannot avoid—though resort to a Fifth Amendment privilege against self-incrimination may not cause the loss of a public position. The rights of an applicant are roughly comparable. As we noted in chapter II, many states have adopted laws that limit the extent to which, and the ways in which, criminal records may be used by government agencies in the hiring process.

### May a public employee or applicant be required to take a polygraph or lie-detector test?

Though polygraph use by private employers was all but eliminated by Congress in 1988,[33] public employees and applicants remain potentially subject to such tests. As recently as December 1991 the Washington Supreme Court held that state agencies may use polygraph tests, even on applicants for clerical positions, if the job involves access to sensitive information and if the scope of inquiry is no broader than necessary to serve the state's interests.[34] The court deferred to the state's asserted interest in "providing its citizens with law enforcement employees of high moral character and integrity"[35]—an interest arguably served by lie-detector testing despite the mounting criticism of both the accuracy and the fairness of such investigatory techniques.

Other courts have been more sensitive to that criticism and to public employee challenges. The Texas Supreme Court recently struck down polygraph use by the state Mental Health Department because the need to provide a safe environment for patients simply did not outweigh the state workers' privacy claims under the state constitution.[36] And the California Supreme Court, which has shaped so much important public employment law, struck down a state polygraph requirement—though primarily because the state law protected not only all private employees but specifically exempted "public safety officers," thus leaving exposed to polygraph use only those people who held less sensitive government jobs.[37] Such an irrational patchwork made it unnecessary to decide the ultimate issue on which the Texas and Washington courts split—a question on which lower federal and state courts remain divided, and which the Supreme Court has not addressed.

## May public employees and applicants be subjected to random drug testing?

The answer depends on many factors, though courts have tended to give agencies latitude in testing programs. As the national concern about drug use and its effects has mounted, the pressure for random, unannounced testing has also grown. The courts have increasingly been drawn into the fray and have faced an increasingly complex set of constitutional questions.

The issue was bound to reach the Supreme Court, and in the spring of 1989 it did—in a pair of cases, one of which involved testing of certain Treasury Department employees (specifically those involved directly in drug enforcement, those who carried firearms, and those who handled "classified" material as part of their duties.) Test results could not be used in a criminal prosecution without the employee's consent; the goals of the program, the Court declared in *National Treasury Employees Union v. Von Raab*,[38] "are to deter drug use among those eligible for promotion to sensitive positions within the service and to prevent the promotion of drug users to those positions."[39]

Such agency interests, said the justices, "present a special need that may justify departure from the ordinary warrant and probable cause requirements,"[40] which the Fourth Amendment would normally impose on any physical search of public workers. The employees did not claim that a warrant need be obtained each time a public worker was tested, nor did the Court find any basis for such a burden. Rather, they argued that the normal search requirements of "probable cause" applied here as well. That claim the majority now rejected: "The Government's need to conduct suspicionless searches . . . outweighs the privacy interests of employees involved in drug enforcement and in carrying firearms."[41] (The third group of target employees—those having access to classified information—could not so readily be assessed, and on that part of the case the Court ordered further consideration.)

The majority's reasoning provides whatever guidance the cases yield. Several factors were vital to the judgment. The Court began by recognizing that under its precedents, compelled drug tests did amount to a search to which Fourth Amendment protections clearly applied. The existence here of an involuntary invasion of personal privacy was beyond dispute. But that was only the start of the inquiry. Paramount on the other side of the constitutionally required balancing was the strength of the governmental interest: "Where, as here, the possible harm against which the Government seeks to guard is substantial, the need to prevent its occurrence furnishes an ample justification for reasonable searches calculated to advance the Government's goal."[42]

Equally critical is the nature of the position: "It is plain that certain forms of public employment may diminish privacy expectations even with respect to personal searches." And as to the jobs targeted for suspicionless drug searches here: "Customs employees who are directly involved in the interdiction of illegal drugs or who are required to carry firearms in the line of duty likewise have a diminished expectation of privacy in respect to the intrusions occasioned by a urine test."[43] Thus the nature of the targeted positions, against which the generalized government goals must be judged, led this Court to sustain the suspicionless, warrantless drug testing. On the other hand, the Court was not fully persuaded of the need when it came to employees with access to "classified" material and sent that part of the case back to lower courts.

If the testing policy covered only those who handled truly sensitive data, the agency interest would be comparable to that involved in drug enforcement and firearms use. But the inclusion in the policy of some seemingly less sensitive jobs—

baggage clerk, messenger, animal caretaker, and the like—raised doubts "whether the Service has defined this category of employees more broadly than necessary to meet [its needs]."[44]

Four members of the Court dissented—Justices Brennan and Marshall, arguing that the Fourth Amendment barred random, suspicionless searches; and Justices Scalia and Stevens, arguing that the government had failed to prove its case in the absence "of even a single instance in which any of the speculated horribles actually occurred."[45] Since that time, of course, two of the dissenters have left the Court. At least one, if not both, of their successors would have joined the majority. Thus the force of the judgment has surely not been diminished by the passage of time.

The lower courts have, however, been fairly strict in their application of the Supreme Court's principles. Many cases have, in fact, rejected claims of government need to use suspicionless, random drug tests. Soon after the Supreme Court spoke, another group of federal workers successfully challenged a similar policy, as applied to all Food and Nutrition Service workers, and won in the federal appeals court.[46] The proper principle here, under the *Treasury Employees* case, was that "the government's legitimate interest in employee drug testing extends no further than its interest in workplace conduct and performance of work responsibilities."[47] Thus the court held the testing program unconstitutional as applied to workers who did not hold safety- or security-sensitive positions, "in the absence of reasonable suspicion of on-duty drug use or drug-impaired work performance."[48]

The court also struck down a provision for visual observation of all employees who were ordered to undergo reasonable-suspicion urinalysis; "we can discern no weighty government interest in observation that counterbalances its intrusion on employee privacy."[49] The appeals court added an ironic note: while the government had earlier defended drug testing as infallible, the basis asserted here in support of the visual observation was concern about the vulnerability of such tests to cheating—a concern quite at variance with the theory the government used a year earlier in convincing the Supreme Court to validate the program. There was more than a hint that Justice Department lawyers could not have it both ways.

The lower courts have focused much more on *Treasury Em-*

*ployees'* exceptions than on its core. Thus federal courts have struck down suspicionless testing of applicants for Justice Department attorney positions that do not involve public safety or handling sensitive information,[50] returning Philadelphia transit workers holding non-safety-sensitive positions,[51] and federal agency operators of motor vehicles who neither carry passengers nor have access to classified information.[52]

The Massachusetts Supreme Judicial Court, in one of the relatively few recent state cases, struck down as unconstitutional a random urinalysis program imposed on all Boston police officers.[53] And another federal appeals court held that a city could require its police officers to undergo drug tests—apart from a uniform or systematic random selection program—only if a given officer were chosen on the basis of "a reasonable suspicion" derived from specific objective facts and inferences from those facts.[54] Thus the singling out of a particular officer for testing on the basis of an unsubstantiated rumor that the officer associated with drug dealers was insufficient and violated the officers's privacy rights. Thus the *Treasury Employees* case may have set the guidelines, but its limitations have initially proved more important than its invitations.

## May public employees be required to meet certain standards for dress, hairstyle, and grooming?

In some respects, and for some positions, the answer is yes, although many matters remain unsettled. The Supreme Court addressed the issue only once and has given partial guidance. In that case, *Kelly v. Johnson*,[55] a group of male police officers objected to a county rule that required them to cut their hair short and took the issue to federal court. The appeals court held that "choice of personal appearance is an ingredient of an individual's personal liberty" and on that basis struck down the rule. But the Supreme Court reversed and upheld the hair length-and-style rules, at least for uniformed police officers. Though conceding that the Constitution does protect a person's choice of personal appearance, the Court deferred to the police rule so long as "any rational connection" could be shown between the challenged policy and "the promotion of safety of persons and property." Such a link was not hard to find— whether in a desire to make police officers readily recognizable to citizens or in "a desire for the esprit de corps that such similarity is felt to inculcate within the police force itself."[56] Justice Powell concurred separately, as was his wont in close cases, wishing to keep open the issue of "a liberty interest within the Fourteenth Amendment as to matters of personal appearance"[57] and thus suggesting that outside the paramilitary uniformed services such rules would likely fare less well.

Under *Kelly*'s "rational relationship" test it is not surprising that some courts and arbitrators have given police and fire departments substantial leeway in regulating hair length and style. The scope of authority has gone beyond facial hair; a federal judge recently rejected the plea of a Montgomery, Alabama, firefighter who was ordered to trim chest hair that protruded from his collar.[58] One federal appeals court has gone so far as to sustain an Illinois town's rule barring police officers from wearing earrings while off duty.[59]

Yet there have been some notable exceptions to this trend— a District of Columbia Superior Court judgment striking down the district's ban on beards worn by firefighters,[60] and judgments favorable to bearded police officers by the New York Port Authority arbitrator[61] and by the Maryland Human Relations Commission.[62] The Maryland case suggests an avenue that may prove more promising for some in the public service—recognition that for certain employees, notably African Americans, sporting a beard may be more than a matter of vanity but may in fact implicate health interests as well. If a hair length-and-style rule can be shown to have—albeit unintended—a racially selective impact, then it may well be vulnerable for reasons that simply were not addressed in the *Kelly* case. And there is always the latent potential of a First Amendment claim that such dimensions of lifestyle as hair length and fashion do represent a constitutionally protected form of expression.

Similar issues have arisen with regard to dress and other aspects of personal appearance. Where the job involves wearing a uniform, the *Kelly* case would appear to validate such standards. Occupations in the public service that demand less uniformity in dress have also been the subject of legal challenge, with less consistent results. A New York state agency upheld the right of a physical education teacher to wear a bikini while teaching swimming,[63] and an arbitrator held that an elementary teacher could not be forbidden to wear a pantsuit in the classroom.[64] Later, however, a federal appeals courts held that a public-school teacher could be denied reemployment at least partly because of the shortness of her skirts, since the attire seemed relevant to her role and her "image," and since the court could find no constitutional basis for protecting the choice of skirt length.[65] Another federal court rejected a male teacher's claim that he could not be reprimanded for refusing to wear a necktie in class as the principal had demanded.[66]

The volume of litigation on this issue has steadily diminished—probably as a result of more relaxed agency policies on dress and grooming. But if and when the issue does reach a court, the quest for constitutional protection of a public employee's preference in dress and grooming remains elusive and uncertain.

### May a public employee be penalized because of heterosexual activity and associations?

The answer is curiously mixed in an area where the Supreme Court has consistently come close to intervening but has never done so. The range and variety of cases span a broad spectrum. At one end, courts have been most sympathetic to the unmarried public employee who spends a single night with an old friend of the opposite sex, also unmarried. At the other end is the case of the married California junior college professor caught with a female student in a car in the college parking lot, *in flagrante delicto.*[67] The hard cases fall between these two extremes. The results are not easily predictable, although a few factors can be identified.

Two federal appeals courts reached contrasting results in a pair of similar cases, among the few recent reported decisions. Two members of the Amarillo (Texas) Police Department, male and female, both unmarried, were suspended (and one of them demoted) for off-duty dating and cohabitation. When they pressed their privacy claims, the federal courts could find no constitutional interest at risk and dismissed the suit.[68] The Supreme Court declined to review the case,[69] although three justices expressed in a dissent their view that such activity was part of the officers' constitutionally protected zone of personal privacy.

The other case involved two employees of a public library in Pennsylvania. A relationship developed between a married male custodian and an unmarried female librarian, which eventually led to the women's pregnancy. Library officials learned of the relationship and demanded that it cease. When the employees refused that order, both were dismissed. They sought aid from the federal courts, where they found a slightly more receptive climate than had the Amarillo police officers, but ultimately fared no better. The district court acknowledged that the scope of constitutional privacy did "encompass and protect the personal intimacies of the home, the family, motherhood, procreation and child rearing."[70] There was no evidence of adverse effect upon the job performance of either former employee. But against the state's claimed desire to protect the integrity of marriage and morality, no constitutional interest was strong enough to set aside the library's action.

The federal appeals court summarily affirmed the dismissal, without even an opinion.[71] This case also went to the Supreme Court, and here too the justices declined review.[72] Justice Marshall, in dissent, argued that the library's action violated a recognized interest in personal privacy; the right of the dismissed employees "to pursue an open, rather than a clandestine, personal relationship, and to rear their child together in this environment" was one which in Marshall's view "closely resemble[d] the other aspects of personal privacy to which we have extended constitutional protection."[73]

In contrast to these judgments, there is the more sensitive view of one other federal appeals court in a case involving a North Muskegon, Michigan, police officer. After having separated from his wife, Officer Briggs began cohabiting with another woman. He reported the relationship, including its sexual intimacies, to his chief. The chief promptly suspended Briggs on suspicion of actions "unbecoming a police officer." After a hearing at which Briggs refused to change his course, he was dismissed. When he took his case to federal court, he found sympathetic judges at both the trial and appellate levels. This time the courts recognized a constitutional right of personal privacy that "extends to sexual conduct in intimate relationships between unmarried individuals." Without extensive discussion of the special needs of public employment, the *Briggs* court simply held in the officer's favor and ordered his reinstatement.[74] Once again the Supreme Court was asked to intervene, but once again declined to do so. This time, a different trio of justices—White, Burger and Rehnquist—dissented. They

argued the Court should take up an issue of obvious importance
to public employees, on which the lower federal courts had
been so badly split. Thus six of the nine Justices during the
1980s had urged the review of at least one such case. But the
requisite four votes needed for such review never converged
in a single case. So the issue thus remains in that confused and
uncertain state where the lower courts have left it.

Despite the lack of clarity in results, a few factors may be
helpful in approaching such issues. Government's interest depends substantially on the basis claimed for an adverse personnel action. So in turn the employee's claim may be stronger if,
as we saw in chapter III, his or her asserted interest is freedom
of association rather than the more abstract and diffuse zone of
personal privacy. Beyond that point, the particular circumstances surely shape the outcome.

Clearly sex flaunted on the job is a special matter, as the
California junior college case recognizes. And where a relationship, even off the job, affects or impairs performance on the
job, the government interest is also stronger. Even where
performance is not directly impaired, there may be a direct
bearing upon morale or efficiency in the workplace—as in the
case of a California teacher who was not only an active member
of a "swingers" club, engaging in intercourse with various men
other than her husband, but who boasted about her exploits on
a television program where fellow teachers recognized her
despite a pseudonym and disguise.[75] The nature of the position
is also surely relevant; in some situations conduct that would
otherwise be tolerated may be found to affect adversely the
employee's fitness for a job the very nature of which demands
a high standard of conduct and propriety. Finally, the fre-
quency and openness or notoriety of the conduct undoubtedly
bears on the judgment; a single and discreet liaison will usually
be tolerated even on the part of one who holds a highly sensitive
and visible position.

## May a person be denied public employment for having a child out of wedlock?

There have been widely publicized cases of unmarried teachers being dismissed for bearing children or even for becoming
pregnant. The Supreme Court agreed in 1976 to review one
such case, but then dismissed it a few months later without

explanation and without any ruling.[76] The lower federal courts had struck down a school board rule that barred the employment of unwed mothers for teaching positions. The district court held that such a policy was "patently absurd" in part because it "equates the single fact of illegitimate birth with irredeemable moral disease," because it required school officials to investigate the parental status of all applicants, and because the schools could if they felt it necessary preserve morality by other and less intrusive means.[77] The court of appeals agreed, finding that the rule bore no rational relationship to the school district's asserted goals.

Such policies have also been drawn in question because they affect women much more harshly than men. Thus a federal court in Indiana ruled in favor of an unmarried female schoolteacher who was not rehired apparently for the sole reason that she had become pregnant during a relationship with a fellow teacher.[78] On preliminary motions, the court ventured that the school authorities may "have intruded on [the teacher's] right to be free from governmental intrusion in making her personal decisions related to marriage, procreation, contraception and child rearing." The judge also felt the teacher might be able to prove a violation both of Title VII of the federal Civil Rights Act (forbidding gender discrimination) and of a state law that barred discrimination "because of marital status." The other cases on this issue have been in conflict, much like the cases that address other facets of heterosexual conduct and activity.

### May a person be denied public employment for being gay or lesbian, or for homosexual associations?

The answer remains surprisingly unclear, at least as far as the courts are concerned. On one hand, a growing number of states—seven at last count—and many cities and counties, as well as the United States civil service system, have laws or policies that forbid discrimination on grounds of sexual preference or orientation, and thus make it unlawful to refuse to hire or otherwise discriminate because a person is gay or lesbian.[79] On the other hand, the United States Defense Department until 1993 maintained a total ban on acceptance of gay and lesbian persons in the armed forces—a policy that the Clinton administration during its first weeks in office pledged to end, and toward the termination of which it took early and major steps. The courts have, despite intense and persistent constitutional challenge, upheld that policy[80] (save in unusual cases where, for example, one of the services has repeatedly reenlisted a person known by it to be homosexual.)[81] Under this policy, more than 13,000 service personnel are reported to have been dismissed in the past decade. Between the military ban on one end, and protective laws on the other, many difficult cases remain for resolution.

A number of state and federal courts have ruled that public employers may not discriminate against persons for being gay or lesbian—from an early and sweeping California Supreme Court judgment in favor of a gay teacher,[82] to quite recent federal court decisions requiring the Dallas Police Department to hire an otherwise fully qualified lesbian as an officer,[83] and finding constitutionally suspect a Kansas public school's refusal to employ a teacher with "homosexual tendencies."[84] Even when dealing with highly sensitive positions, courts have called agencies to account, as one federal judge recently did in requiring the FBI to demonstrate at least a rational basis for revoking the security clearance of a gay agent who alleged his homosexuality was the bureau's only concern.[85]

On the other hand, there are cases (even quite recent) to the contrary. The Washington State Supreme Court in 1977 upheld the dismissal by a high school of a "known homosexual".[86] That court accepted without question a finding by the trial judge that the mere fact of being gay, if known within the school, "impaired" the teacher's efficiency. And as recently as 1990 a federal appeals court sustained the Defense Department's policy of subjecting gay applicants for secret and top-secret security clearances to a higher level of scrutiny and a much more onerous review process. The district judge had found in favor of the gay and lesbian applicants.

The appeals court reversed, however, and rejected the full range of constitutional claims advanced by the clearance-seekers, in *High Tech Gays v. Defense Industrial Security Clearance Office*.[87] This opinion stressed the Supreme Court's 1986 judgment upholding the constitutionality of state sodomy laws[88]—a judgment that to this court seemed to removed the underpinning of claims that other courts had accepted on behalf of gay and lesbian public workers. It could find no other basis for the claim that "homosexual conduct is a protected fundamental right". One other premise of this judgment—that "homosexuality is not an immutable characteristic [like] . . . race, gender or alienage" has been directly challenged by very recent medical findings about physical differences between gay and nongay males;[89] such evidence bears directly on the public employment issue and will surely be brought into the litigation process in the very near future.

Meanwhile, several possibly helpful factors have emerged from the cases:

First, the public or private nature of a person's sexual preference may be relevant. Courts have in practice drawn distinctions between private and discreet homosexuality, and those who have flaunted or widely publicized their preference. The Civil Service Policy denies its protection in cases where "notoriety" may impair a person's fitness.

Second, the nature of the position is sometimes relevant; courts have been more deferential to agencies that are concerned about homosexuality in highly sensitive or security-prone positions, as with a recent federal appeals court judgment upholding the dismissal of a state university police officer for suspected homosexual activity in campus rest rooms.[90]

Third, there has been least sympathy for the public worker who misrepresents his or her preference—as with a Maryland teacher who persuaded a court that the school's bias against gay persons was invalid, but still lost his case because he had lied to school authorities about his homosexuality when he was hired.[91] Even though sympathetic to the consequences of making full disclosure, this court nonetheless sustained the action on grounds of integrity rather than sexual orientation.

Given such limited guidance, the issue remains surprisingly open. Despite impressions (and even headlines) to the contrary, the Supreme Court has repeatedly refused to intervene in homosexual public employment cases such as that of the Washington State gay teacher and an Ohio school guidance counselor who was dismissed after telling co-workers she was bisexual. The High Court has, however, contributed one marginally helpful and pertinent judgment: By an equal division, with Justice Powell taking no part in the case, it affirmed in 1985 the judgment of a lower court that Oklahoma schoolteachers cannot be discharged for speaking out in favor of gay rights, regardless of their own sexual preference or orientation.[92] That judgment is, of course, a much easier one on familiar free speech grounds of the kind we studied back in chapter III. It is the equal protection claims on behalf of gay and lesbian public workers that remain complex and confusing.

## May public workers be subjected to mandatory testing for AIDS?

The status of AIDS in the workplace is rapidly changing and is the subject of much attention and discussion. While more than half the states do protect (under disability or handicap discrimination laws) persons with HIV infection, such protection is far from universal.[93] A few courts have already shown some sympathy to the employment claims of persons with AIDS. Thus in July 1992 a federal judge in Washington held that the District of Columbia could not refuse to hire a firefighter because he was HIV-infected.[94] Basing that judgment on the federal Rehabilitation Act (which we will examine more closely in chapter VI), the court found that employing an HIV-infected person posed "no measurable risk," since he could not transmit the disease to others in the line of duty. The court also ordered the district to pay $25,000 in damages to the rejected firefighter for "emotional pain and suffering" caused by an act of intentional and forbidden discrimination. The decision presumably applies to virtually all public occupations, save perhaps for those in which a risk of transmission exists and thus poses a danger to the health of fellow workers or clients of the agency. It is too early to tell whether this judgment and the few others like it will establish a pattern of judicial protection where statutory safeguards are unclear.

In this uncertain environment, the question of required AIDS testing becomes critical. Only a few courts have addressed the issue. One federal judge upheld the policies of Willoughby, Ohio, in requiring firefighters and paramedics to be tested for AIDS; the city had asserted not only a valid interest but in fact "a legal duty to protect its residents from contracting the HIV virus from such high risk employees" and thus did not violate their Fourth Amendment privacy interests by mandating such tests.[95] Earlier, a federal judge in Virginia had rejected the constitutional claim of a civilian employee of the army who objected to having been AIDS-tested as part of a battery of blood presurgery blood tests following a serious injury.[96] That court found no violation of privacy, since the employee had consented to testing for other purposes, and since a government agency about to perform surgery had a compelling interest in knowing whether a patient was HIV-infected. Similarly, a federal judge in Louisiana held that state hospital officials had a legitimate need to test for AIDS a known homosexual nurse who refused testing after his male roommate died of AIDS.[97] The court actually sustained the nurse's discharge because he had failed to disclose the result of an earlier AIDS test and had concealed prior infections in violation of hospital rules. The court added that given the hospital's widely publicized infection control policies, an employee who worked with patients could have had no reasonable expectations of privacy against required testing.

The major case to the contrary arose in Nebraska and involved a group of mental retardation agency employees. The agency had required all persons working with mentally retarded clients to submit to blood testing for AIDS (as well as hepatitis). The employees challenged the policy in federal court and prevailed at both the trial and appellate levels. The district court began by declaring that mandatory drug testing was clearly a search governed by Fourth Amendment principles. It then applied the balancing test which the Supreme Court announced in the *Ortega* (desk search) case. That test required the agency to show an interest sufficient to overcome the employee's reasonable expectations of privacy. The agency argued that a lower standard should apply here because its clients were a particularly susceptible population. But the trial judge rejected that claim, finding that the risk of transmission to patients was "minuscule, trivial, extremely low . . . and approaches zero."[98] The appeals court agreed and held that the AIDS-testing program "is not reasonable at its inception under Fourth Amendment standards" because the "agency's articulated interest in requiring testing does not constitutionally justify requiring employees to submit to a test for the purpose of protecting the clients from an infected employee."[99]

There is one important caveat: this judgment preceded by several months the Supreme Court's drug-testing decisions. Although the lower court conscientiously applied the same constitutional formula that governed the drug-testing cases, the High Court's approach in sustaining the challenged drug tests may now complicate the task of public workers like those who successfully attacked the Nebraska AIDS-testing program. Clearly there must be many more cases, and probably review by the Supreme Court, before one invokes the Nebraska precedent with continued confidence.

## NOTES

1. *National Treasury Employees Union v. Von Raab*, 489 U.S. 656 (1989).
2. *E.g., Anonymous Fireman v. City of Willloughby*, 779 F. Supp. 402 (N.D. Ohio 1991).
3. *O'Connor v. Ortega*, 480 U.S. 709 (1987).
4. *Id.* at 715.
5. *Id.*
6. *Id.* at 716.
7. *Id.* at 717.
8. *Id.* at 718.
9. *Id.*
10. *Id.* at 719–20.
11. *Id.* at 720.
12. *Id.* at 726.
13. *Id.*
14. *Id.*
15. *Id.*
16. *American Postal Workers' Union v. United States Postal Service*, 871 F.2d 556 (6th Cir. 1989).
17. *Chicago Fire Fighters Union Local 2 v. Chicago*, 717 F. Supp. 1314 (N.D. Ill. 1989).
18. *Bateman v. Florida*, 513 So. 2d 1101 (Fla. Dist. Ct. App. 1987).
19. *Fraternal Order of Police Lodge No. 5 v. Philadelphia*, 859 F.2d 276 (3d Cir. 1988).
20. Washington Post, May 1, 1992, at A25, col. 1.
21. *Gayer v. Schlesinger*, 490 F.2d 740, 751 (D.C. Cir. 1973).
22. *Gayer v. Laird*, 332 F. Supp. 169, 171 (D.D.C. 1971).
23. *Scott v. Macy*, 402 F.2d 644, 648 (D.C. Cir. 1968).
24. *Anonymous v. Kissinger*, 499 F.2d 1097, 1102 (D.C. Cir. 1974).
25. Pub. L. No. 93–579, 88 Stat. 1896 (1974) (codified as 5 U.S.C. §§ 552 A *et seq.* (1988)).
26. 5 U.S.C. § 552 A(g)(4) (1988).
27. *Fraternal Order of Police Lodge No. 5 v. Philadelphia*, 859 F.2d 276 (3d Cir. 1988).

28. *Carmel by the Sea v. Young*, 2 Cal. 3d 259, 466 P.2d 225, 85 Cal. Rptr. 1 (1970).

29. *E.g., Montgomery County v. Walsh*, 274 Md. 489, 336 A.2d 97 (1975); *Illinois State Employees Association v. Walker*, 57 Ill. 2d 512, 315 N.E.2d 9 (1974).

30. *Gardner v. Broderick*, 392 U.S. 273, 278 (1968).

31. *Slochower v. Board of Education*, 350 U.S. 551 (1956).

32. *Uniformed Sanitationmen's Association v. Commissioner of Sanitation*, 392 U.S. 280 (1968).

33. Employee Polygraph Protection Act of 1988, Pub. L. No. 100–347, 102 Stat. 646 (1988) (codified as 29 U.S.C. §§ 2001 *et seq.* (1988)).

34. *O'Hartigan v. Washington Department of Personnel*, 118 Wash. 2d 111, 821 P.2d 44 (1991); *see also Anderson v. Philadelphia*, 845 F.2d 1216 (3d Cir. 1988).

35. *O'Hartigan v. Washington Department of Personnel*, 821 P.2d at 49.

36. *Texas State Employees Union v. Texas Department of Mental Health and Mental Retardation*, 31 Tex. Sup. Ct. J. 33, 746 S.W.2d 203 (1987).

37. *Long Beach City Employees Association v. City of Long Beach*, 41 Cal. 3d 937, 719 P.2d 660, 227 Cal. Rptr. 90 (1986).

38. *National Treasury Employees Union v. Von Raab*, 489 U.S. 656 (1989).

39. *Id.*

40. *Id.*

41. *Id.* at 668.

42. *Id.* at 675.

43. *Id.* at 672.

44. *Id.* at 675.

45. *Id.* at 683.

46. *Treasury Employees v. Yeutter*, 918 F.2d 968 (D.C. Cir. 1990).

47. *Id.* at 974.

48. *Id.*

49. *Id.* at 975.

50. *Willner v. Thornburgh*, 928 F.2d 1185 (D.C. Cir. 1991).

51. *Bolden v. Southeastern Pennsylvania Transportation Authority*, 953 F.2d 807 (3d Cir. 1991).

52. *American Federation of Government Employees v. Sullivan*, 787 F. Supp. 255 (D.D.C. 1992).

53. *Guiney v. Police Commissioner of Boston*, 411 Mass. 328, 582 N.E.2d 523 (1991).

54. *Ford v. Dowd*, 931 F.2d 1286 (8th Cir. 1991); *Jackson v. Gates*, 975 F.2d 648 (9th Cir. 1992).

55. 425 U.S. 238 (1976).

56. *Id.* at 248.

57. *Id.* at 244.

58. New York Times, June 27, 1992, at 11, col. 6.

59. *Rathert v. Village of Peotone*, 903 F.2d 510 (7th Cir. 1990).

60. Washington Post, Oct. 29, 1991, at B5, cols. 1–3.

61. New York Times, Jan. 4, 1987, sec. 1, at 31 col. 6.

62. New York Times, Feb. 1, 1991, at A16, col. 6.

63. *Matter of Heather Martin*, No. 8156 (N.Y. Commissioner of Education, August 31, 1971).

64. *In re School District of Kingsley and Kingsley Board of Education Association*, 56 Lab. Arb. 1138 (1971).

65. *East Hartford Education Association v. Board of Education of East Hartford*, 562 F.2d 838 (2d Cir. 1977).

66. *Carter v. United States*, 407 F.2d 1238 (D.C. Cir. 1968).

67. *Board of Trustees v. Stubblefield*, 16 Cal. App. 3d 820, 94 Cal. Rptr. 318 (1971).

68. *Shawgo v. Spradlin*, 701 F.2d 470 (5th Cir. 1983).

69. *Shawgo v. Spradlin*, 701 F.2d 740 (5th Cir.) *cert. denied sub nom. Whisenhunt v. Spradlin*, 464 U.S. 965 (1983).

70. *Hollenbaugh v. Carnegie Free Library*, 405 F. Supp. 629 (W.D. Pa. 1975), 436 F. Supp. 1328 (W.D. Pa. 1977).

71. 578 F.2d 1374 (3rd Cir. 1978).

72. 439 U.S. 1052 (1978).

73. *Id.* at 1055.

74. *Briggs v. North Muskegon Police Department*, 563 F. Supp. 585 (W.D. Mich. 1983), *aff'd*, 746 F.2d 1475 (7th Cir. 1984, *cert. denied*, 473 U.S. 909 (1985).

75. *Pettit v. State Board of Education*, 10 Cal. 3d 29, 513 P. 2d 889, 109 Cal. Rptr. 665 (1973).

76. *Andrews v. Drew Municipal Separate School District*, 507 F.2d 611 (5th Cir. 1975).

77. *Id.*

78. *Clark v. Hamilton Community Schools*, Civil No. F84–136 (N.D. Ind. 1985) (available on LEXIS).

79. *See generally, The Rights of Lesbians and Gay Men: ACLU Guide to a Gay Person's Rights*, 3d ed. (1992).

80. *E.g., Dronenberg v. Zech*, 741 F.2d 1388 (D.C. Cir. 1984).

81. *Watkins v. United States Army*, 875 F.2d 699 (9th Cir. 1989).

82. *Morrison v. State Board of Education*, 1 Cal. 3d 214, 461 P.2d 375, 82 Cal. Rptr. 175 (1969); *see also Norton v. Macy*, 417 F.2d 1161 (D.C. Cir 1969).

83. See New York Times, Feb. 5, 1992, at A17, col. 1–4.

84. *Jantz v. Muci*, 759 F. Supp. 1543, 1545 (D. Kan. 1991), *rev'd on*

grounds of qualified governmental immunity, 976 F.2d 623 (10th Cir. 1992).

85. *Buttino v. Federal Bureau of Investigation*, 801 F. Supp. 298 (N.D. Cal. 1992).

86. *Gaylord v. Tacoma School District No. 10*, 88 Wash. 2d 286, 559 P.2d 1340, *cert. denied*, 434 U.S. 879 (1977).

87. 895 F.2d 563 (9th Cir. 1990).

88. *Bowers v. Hardwick*, 478 U.S. 186 (1986).

89. See Washington Post, Aug. 1, 1992, at A2, cols. 4–5.

90. *Delahoussaye v. City of New Iberia*, 937 F.2d 144 (5th Cir. 1991).

91. *Acanfora v. Board of Education*, 491 F.2d 498 (4th Cir. 1974).

92. *National Gay Task Force v. Board of Education*, 729 F.2d 1270 (10th Cir. 1984), *aff'd by an equally divided Court*, 470 U.S. 903 (1985).

93. See Note, 52 *U. Pitt. L. Rev.* 327 (1991); Note, 90 *Colum. L. Rev.* 720 (1990).

94. *Doe v. District of Columbia*, 1992 U.S. Dist. Lexis 9168 (D.D.C. July 1, 1992).

95. *Anonymous Fireman v. City of Willoughby*, 779 F. Supp. 402 (N.D. Ohio 1991).

96. *Plowman v. United States Army*, 698 F. Supp. 627 (E.D. Va. 1988).

97. *Leckelt v. Board of Hospital Commissioners*, 909 F.2d 820 (5th Cir. 1990).

98. *Glover v. Eastern Nebraska Community Office of Retardation*, 686 F. Supp. 243, 251 (D. Neb. 1988).

99. 867 F.2d 461, 464 (8th Cir.), *cert. denied*, 493 U.S. 932 (1989).

# VI

# Race, Gender, and
# Disability Discrimination

What can public employees do about discrimination on
grounds of race, gender, or disability? Today such forms of bias
are all but completely forbidden in the public workplace. But
it has not always been so. In fact, until the Civil Rights Act of
1991[1] many thousands of federal workers and several major
groups of state and local employees were not protected by the
antidiscrimination laws that covered virtually all other workers
in the nation. And even where coverage is clear, some major
uncertainties about the scope of remedies remain. Not until
1992 did the Supreme Court recognize that a female public
worker who had been the victim of sex discrimination in violation of Title VI of the Civil Rights Act could obtain damages
from her employer.[2] Thus the law in this area is constantly
evolving, probably more rapidly than in any other facet of
public employment.

**What laws protect public employees from race discrimi-
nation?**
Though most states have adopted antidiscrimination laws
that cover public as well as private workers, our main focus is
on that body of federal law that affords the broadest protection.
The evolution of those safeguards goes back to the year after
the Civil War, when Congress enacted the earliest civil rights
laws. Section 1981 of that law grants to all persons the same
right to make and enforce contracts as had been enjoyed by
white citizens.[3] This provision was early held to cover employment because a contract is clearly involved. Another post-Civil
War law, Section 1983,[4] gives a remedy to any person who has
been deprived of his or her civil rights by any other person
"acting under color of state law." Since a state or local government agency or official clearly acts "under color of state law",
this provision also applies to public employees.

Substantial protection did not come until Congress, a century
later, adopted the Civil Rights Act of 1964.[5] Title VII of that

law forbids discrimination in employment on the basis of race, color, religion, or national origin. At first, Title VII applied only to private employers. Then in 1972, Congress added section 717, which extended protection to most federal employees.[6] Most state and local workers are also covered—though, as we shall see, the remedies and procedures open to nonfederal employees differ somewhat. At first it was unclear whether federal workers could still invoke the older civil rights laws as well. In 1976 the Supreme Court held that Section 717 afforded federal workers an exclusive remedy for employment discrimination and thus barred resort to Sections 1981 and 1983;[7] the options open to state and local employees are less clear.

Title VII contained some important gaps in its coverage. More than seven thousand employees of the United States Senate and many political appointees in the Executive Branch simply were not covered until Congress included them within the Civil Rights Act of 1991,[8] filling that gap and establishing a new and different procedure for handling such discrimination complaints. Also protected for the first time by the 1991 amendments were persons who hold policymaking positions on the staffs of state and local elected officials, and persons serving such officials as "immediate advisors with respect to the exercise of the constitutional or legal powers of the office."[9] Thus two major gaps in the prior law were at last plugged, giving virtually complete coverage of the public sector workforce.

### Who is protected by these anti-discrimination laws?
Although the post-Civil War laws were designed to protect the rights of former slaves, they were later extended to other racial minorities—Hispanics, Asian Americans, Pacific Islanders, and Native Americans—who may also be victims of discrimination. Title VII from the start reached all such racial minority groups.

An increasingly difficult question has been the degree to which these laws protect nonminority persons. The Supreme Court substantially resolved that issue in 1976 by holding that whites as well as blacks and other minorities could be victims of discrimination on the basis of race[10] and thus might seek legal recourse. The Court found Title VII's goal to be banning any discrimination on the basis of race or color, whichever way it ran. In practice such claims are rare; the federal Equal Employment Opportunity Commission recently noted that only 3 percent of its cases are brought by white workers, despite the coverage of the laws it administers.[11] The complex related issues of affirmative action and preferential hiring—and their effect on nonminorities —are discussed later in this chapter.

**What forms of employment discrimination are forbidden?**
Most clearly unlawful is refusal or denial of initial employment. Failure to promote a qualified person because of race, or refusal to consider that person on an equal footing with persons of other races are also forbidden. Unequal compensation and differential salary or wage levels are also proscribed. The practical problem is that racial discrimination, even in initial hiring, usually takes forms much subtler than the once infamous "no ———'s need apply." For example, the use of certain tests or educational or experience requirements can have a racially disparate effect, whether or not intended, and often far harder to detect or assess.

Several troublesome issues of coverage and scope were resolved by Congress in the Civil Rights Act of 1991. Courts had construed Section 1981 to forbid only racial bias in hiring and sometimes in promotions but had refused to apply it to such practices as racial harassment in the workplace. The new law clarifies that the basic right of all persons to make employment contracts, clearly protected by Section 1981, now includes the "enjoyment of all benefits, privileges, terms and conditions of the contractual relationship."[12] This expansion brings the force of Section 1981 to bear on harassment and other discriminatory practices that deny equality in the work place.

The 1991 amendments also address the issue of testing, which had been the subject of extensive litigation.[13] Some agencies and employers had adjusted test scores in an effort to give preference to lower-scoring applicant groups. The new Act makes it unlawful for an employer to adjust test scores, use different cut-off scores, or alter the results of job-related tests on the basis of race, color, religion, sex or national origin—a proscription that (for reasons we shall see a bit later) may hamper some affirmative action efforts.[14]

**What process should a victim of federal employment discrimination follow?**
Such a person should first contact the Equal Employment

Opportunity counselor at the agency where the discrimination is alleged to have occurred. If the counselor cannot achieve a satisfactory resolution, the complainant may then seek an administrative hearing before a civil service examiner, who will make a recommendation to the agency head based on the hearing and an independent examination of the complaint. The agency head then decides and informs the complainant. If the complainant is not satisfied, there are two options—bringing suit in federal district court or appealing to the Merit Systems Protection Board. If the complainant takes the latter course, and if the board either fails to act within a prescribed time or rejects the claim, suit may still be brought in federal court.

## What options are available to a state or local employee?

Apart from any state antidiscrimination laws that may exist, an aggrieved state or local worker may pursue claims under Sections 1981 or 1983. If a nonfederal employee wishes to invoke Title VII, however, the process is more complex. Where the state has its own civil rights agency, the employee must go there first and give that agency 60 days to resolve the issue before seeking federal relief. After that time, or if the state agency refuses to act, the claim may be taken to the federal Equal Employment Opportunity Commission. If the state does not have a civil rights agency of its own, the employee must file a complaint with the EEOC within 180 days of the alleged discrimination. And before bringing suit in federal court, the complainant must obtain a "right to sue" letter from the EEOC—which one may demand after the matter has been at least 180 days before the EEOC, or if the Commission has within that time period rejected the claim.

Because of the complex interaction of different levels of jurisdiction and remedies, the best course may be for a state or local employee challenging discrimination to file state and federal claims at the same time—making sure the EEOC is informed that a state claim is also pending. Thus if the EEOC fails to complete action on the case within the 180-day period—which is unlikely to happen—the issue can proceed on a relatively fast track. Since many such cases involve complex factual issues that need detailed investigation prior to litigation, such expeditious procedure is valuable.

One major procedural issue—whether a jury trial is appro-

priate in Title VII cases—has now been resolved by Congress.
The 1991 Civil Rights Act reverses the position taken by many
federal courts during the 1980s, denying a jury trial, and enti-
tles either party to a trial by jury in a Title VII lawsuit.[15]

### What must a complainant prove in a race discrimination case?

A complaining employee must establish at least these elements to sustain a discrimination claim: (1) that he or she
belongs to a protected group; (2) that he or she applied for the
job and was qualified for it; (3) that despite these qualifications,
he or she was denied the job (or was passed over for a promotion
or other benefit); and (4) that after the rejection, the employer
continued to seek applications from other people with the complainant's qualifications.[16]

More common (and usually more effective) than individual
employee complaints are suits on behalf of classes of employees
or applicants alleging that an employer practice discriminates
against, or has disparate impact upon, a protected employee
group. Such suits may challenge tests or other initial requirements for hiring. The basic rule governing such challenges was
one the Supreme Court announced in the *Duke Power* case in
1971—that an employment practice or requirement is discriminatory and therefore invalid if it "operates to exclude [protected
groups and] cannot be shown to be related to job performance."[17] The Court found no need to prove an intent or
purpose to discriminate; it was enough—at least under Title
VII—that the practice be shown to have a racially disparate
impact. (Where a claim is based on the Constitution's Equal
Protection Clause, the Court later held that a racially discriminatory motive or purpose must be shown.)

The justices took special note of two specific types of possible
entry barriers: "Diplomas and tests are useful servants, but
Congress has mandated the commonsense proposition that they
are not to become masters of reality."[18] Since the *Duke Power*
case, many lower courts have refined the test and have insisted
that agencies "validate" employment criteria. Validation is a
quite complex process and was the subject of a detailed set of
EEOC guidelines issued in 1978 that outline several approaches an agency or employer might take to validation.[19]

Many employment criteria have been found discriminatory under the validation process, while few have been sustained.

The 1991 Civil Rights Act has added some clarity on one of the major procedural issues in Title VII litigation. The new law effectively overruled a 1989 Supreme Court case[20] and allocated the burden of proof regarding claims of disparate impact in a way that significantly benefits employee-plaintiffs.[21] Even if the employee demonstrated that a practice has a racially disparate impact, the Supreme Court ruled that the burden remained with the plaintiff. Under the 1991 amendments, the burden shifts at this point: the employer must then prove that the racially disparate practice is "job related for the position in question and consistent with business necessity." Obviously, meeting that test poses a major hurdle for the employer and explains why the allocation of the burden of proof in such a case will often determine the outcome.

The new law alters the burden of proof in another way that favors plaintiffs. The Supreme Court had ruled that when employment decisions reflected "mixed motives"—discriminatory and benign—the employer would win if it could prove the adverse decision would have been made even in the absence of any racial animus.[22] Congress reversed that rule and the law now permits an employee to prevail by proving that racial discrimination was one of the motives, even if others were present and may have shaped the decision.

**If unlawful discrimination is proved, what remedies are available?**

The remedies are generally of four types: (1) an order to hire, rehire, or promote the employee(s) against whom discrimination has been practiced; (2) an injunction against the repetition or continuation of the practice found to be discriminatory; (3) an award of back pay or actual wages the victim(s) would have earned had the discrimination not occurred; and (4) in exceptional cases, an award of punitive damages against an employer found to have discriminated in bad faith. The law also now provides for payment of expert witnesses in Title VII suits.

**May a public employee ever recover punitive damages from the government?**

No. Earlier cases found authority under sections 1981 and

1983 to award damages that went beyond simply back pay or actual loss. Such recovery would be against the individual agency official who took the discriminatory action, and not against the government or the agency itself. The availability of punitive damages against the government had always seemed unlikely under Title VII,[23] and that door was finally shut by Congress in the Civil Rights Act of 1991.[24]

### Are seniority systems invalid if they disadvantage minority groups?

Possibly. Where seniority systems exist by agreement between an employer and a union or employee organization, questions may arise about their fairness or possible racial bias. In bad times, with substantial reductions of the workforce, even a normally benign seniority system may operate in ways that harm minorities, simply because they are likely to be less well represented among the longest-term employees. At the very least, a seniority system must be shown to have been adopted in good faith. Beyond that point, the questions are extremely difficult and complex. Further litigation will be needed to resolve the remaining issues.

### What laws protect public employees against sex or gender discrimination?

The basic sources of such protection are similar to those that address race discrimination. They include Section 1983 of the post-Civil War laws, which forbids discrimination on the basis of gender as well as race and reaches all actions "under color of state law." The core safeguard is Title VII of the 1964 Civil Rights Act,[25] which was extended generally to public employment in 1972 and in 1991 was given broader coverage of previously exempted federal and state positions. This law bars discrimination on ground of sex, save where gender is a "bona fide occupational qualification" for the position in question.[26]

Also important is the Equal Pay Act of 1963, which in principle guarantees equal compensation for equal work.[27] Under this law, employers must compensate people equally, regardless of gender, for tasks that require the same skill, effort, qualifications, and responsibility. The coverage of the Equal Pay Act is, however, incomplete within the public service. In the federal government, it covers civilians in the military services, employees of any executive agency, civil service positions in the legislative or judicial branches, the Postal Service, Library of Congress, and a few other small areas. At the state and local level, all workers are covered except those who are exempt from the civil service, or who either hold an elective office or are personal staff members or legal advisers to, or policymaking officers appointed by, elected officials. Thus the bulk of federal employment and virtually all state and local jobs are covered.

In 1978 Congress added the Pregnancy Discrimination Act,[28] which clarifies that acts of discrimination barred by Title VII include policies that disadvantage women "because of or on the basis of pregnancy, childbirth, or related medical conditions."

In addition, most states have gender discrimination laws of their own, as do many cities and counties. The coverage of such laws varies widely, and for that reason we concentrate here (as we did with regard to race) on the federal system of protection.

## Does the Constitution forbid sex discrimination?

Yes, but much less race discrimination. The Supreme Court has long viewed as "suspect" all classifications and distinctions based on race and has subjected them to strict scrutiny. Distinctions based on gender have been less rigorously tested, under a standard of "middle level scrutiny." While invalidating much sex discrimination, the Supreme Court has sustained differential treatment of men and women in regard to Social Security benefits, exemptions from property taxation, estate proceedings, promotion in the armed forces, and other matters.[29] Even in the course of striking down an Oklahoma law that allowed women to buy beer at age eighteen but required men to be twenty-one, the most the Court would require was that such a legal distinction need "closely serve" a valid state interest.[30] The Equal Rights Amendment, which would have given gender equality a constitutional basis, ultimately failed of passage after many years of advocacy and effort.

## What "bona fide occupational qualifications" (BFOQ) will permit a public employer to differentiate on the basis of gender?

Title VII allows employers to treat men and women differently if the nature of the job so requires. The Equal Employment Opportunity Commission has issued a set of guidelines defining this BFOQ. The guidelines declare that business necessity only, not merely business convenience or employer, customer, or co-worker preference (or aversion), will justify such distinctions. Any differential treatment must be judged not on the basis of "stereotyped characterization of the sexes" or of "characteristics generally attributed to the group" but only on the basis of the "individual capacities" of the particular applicant or employee.

Moreover, when gender is asserted as a bona fide occupational qualification, it must be justified in terms of the specific requirements of a particular job and not on the basis of a general principle or policy such as the desirability of spreading or apportioning tasks within the workplace. Thus, quite clearly, gender may not be the basis for hiring only women as flight attendants, and a broad category of jobs once exclusively female has been opened to men as well.

The Supreme Court's clearest pronouncement is the 1977 case of *Dothard v. Rawlinson*,[31] which we examined in chapter II. The Court struck down Alabama's height and weight requirements for the hiring of prison guards because they had the effect of barring 40 percent of otherwise qualified female applicants but only 1 percent of the male applicants. In the Court's view, the state had failed to demonstrate the need for a certain physical size, in contrast to strength or agility, to perform routine guard duties. Thus male gender could not be a bona fide occupational qualification—directly or, as here, indirectly. The force of this case was qualified by a corollary holding that Alabama could refuse to hire women for sometime violent "contact" duty in maximum security all-male prisons. In that limited situation, the Court acknowledged that male gender could constitute a BFOQ—one of the very few cases in which such a differential has been upheld.

Under the BFOQ standards, courts and agencies have struck down some laws that were designed—sometimes for good motives—to "protect" female employees. Under the EEOC guidelines, for example, gender will not justify limiting access of women to certain jobs on the basis of loads that must be lifted or carried, or for denying to women certain jobs that have traditionally been thought "dangerous" or "unfeminine." Many such laws and policies have been tested and, almost without exception, have been found to violate Title VII without BFOQ justification.

The most recent and clearest example of this scrutiny is the Supreme Court's 1991 decision in the private employment *Johnson Controls* case.[32] Lower courts had divided on the validity of employer fetal-protection policies, which typically barred women of childbearing age from certain jobs or tasks (such as those involving substantial exposure to lead) that were thought to pose a special risk during pregnancy. Female workers filed suit against a private employer, claiming the policy amounted to sex discrimination in violation of Title VII. The lower federal courts rejected that claim, but the Supreme Court reversed, citing the Pregnancy Discrimination Act in applying Title VII. The employer's only possible justification for such a gender-based policy would have been a showing that reproductive capacity is a bona fide occupational qualification. The safety of persons other than the employee could be taken into account in Title VII BFOQ cases, the Court noted—as with the Alabama prison guard case—but only when the classification went to the core of the employee's job performance and related to the central mission of the workplace.

Since in this situation pregnancy did not interfere with a worker's ability to carry out her tasks, the classification was not a BFOQ and was thus in violation of Title VII. The Court did leave open the possibility that such a policy might fare better if it were shown to be the only way in which an employer could protect against a prohibitive risk of civil liability for an occupational hazard such as lead exposure on the job.

### What about "nepotism" laws that bar the employment of both spouses in the same agency?

Laws that bar hiring two spouses in the same agency are often justified on the asserted basis of integrity in order to avoid possible conflicts of interest or real or apparent favoritism. Where one spouse is the agency head or supervisor, such concerns may be valid. But such laws are sometimes applied simply to forbid the employment of both spouses in junior positions. These laws often disadvantage women—sometimes explicitly, by requiring that the wife resign when nepotism occurs, or more often indirectly by denying opportunity to wives in disproportionate numbers.

Such policies could be shown to violate Title VII for that reason and (save in the direct conflict-of-interest situation) would seem to reflect no BFOQ. One federal court has recently so held and even found unconstitutional a New Jersey policy that barred the employment of both spouses in a government agency.[33] An earlier federal case sustained a nepotism bar only because in a small public school system one spouse, as an administrator, had direct supervisory responsibility over the other spouse, a classroom teacher.[34]

### Do mandatory maternity-leave policies constitute unlawful sex discrimination?

Yes, if they do not provide for individualized, case-by-case determinations. The Supreme Court in 1974 held unconstitutional public school maternity-leave policies that required teachers to take leave five months before the expected birth of a child and barred them from returning to the classroom for five months after the birth.[35] Such policies were based on the claimed need to keep unfit teachers out of the classroom and to maintain the continuity of instruction. But the Court found that both interests were ill served by such policies. Since many teachers were entirely fit to teach well after the fifth month, the school board's valid interest in fitness could be better served by judging the individual capacity of each pregnant teacher. As for continuity of instruction, the match was even worse.

The challenged policy might actually run counter to the school's claimed needs, since the required leave date might fall in the middle of a term or even a week. Again a more flexible policy would not only better serve the teacher's needs but would at least as effectively meet the school's interests. Much the same could be said of the return-to-work policies following child birth; again the interests both of teacher and of school called for an individual determination of fitness and capacity and not blanket policies that were unfair to many and therefore discriminatory.

### What procedure should a public employee follow in a case of alleged sex discrimination?

For a federal worker, the procedure under Title VII is essentially the same as the one described earlier for claims of race discrimination. This procedure begins with an appeal inside the agency, after which the employee may go to the Merit Systems Protection Board and eventually to a federal court. For state employees, the procedure under Title VII is more complex, as we saw earlier, though state and local employees (unlike federal workers) may go directly to court if they wish to file suit under Section 1983. Under the Equal Pay Act, an employee claiming discrimination should contact a local office of the Wage and Hour Division of the United States Labor Department, which has responsibility for enforcing the Act. The division will typically investigate, protecting the anonymity of the complainant.

If it finds discrimination, the division will then bring suit against the employer. As an alternative, an individual who wishes may bring suit directly against the agency without going first to the Labor Department. Such a suit must be filed within two years (or if the discrimination is "willful," within three years).

## What must an employee prove to sustain a sex discrimination charge?

As in race-bias cases, an employee must show that she or he was qualified for the position, that despite such qualification the job or promotion was denied, and that the agency continued thereafter to seek applications from persons of the other gender. Proof of a disproportionate impact on one gender will shift the burden of proof—as when the Alabama prison guard standards were shown to bar 40 percent of otherwise qualified women but only 1 percent of men.[36] The agency must then demonstrate the validity of the rules—that is, by proving them essential to the performance of the job—in much the same way race-differential standards may be validated and in ways similar to the BFOQ analysis we explored earlier.

Claims of discrimination may relate to matters other than hiring, promotion, or compensation, though the proof process is similar. A common legal setting is claims of alleged sexual harassment—unlawful when it involves unwelcome sexual advances, requests for sexual favors, or inappropriate sexual conduct—and even purely verbal harassment if the offensive language is used in the presence of, or is directed against, the

complainant because of gender. But an agency is not necessarily
culpable simply because language to which an employee of
either sex objects is freely used in the workplace.

Under the Equal Pay Act, a complainant or class must prove
that men and women are compensated differently for doing comparable tasks in the same agency. The jobs must require equal
skill, effort, and responsibility (each element to be examined separately). The tasks must be performed under similar working
conditions. And the tasks themselves must be substantially similar, even if not identical, to support a claim that different pay
levels violate the Act. If any one of these tests is not met, the
employer has not violated the Equal Pay Act—though an employer may not avoid such a claim simply by reducing male compensation to create an artificial parity of pay levels.

The employer can answer an Equal Pay charge by showing
that differentials are the result of a seniority system, a merit system, or a "system which measures earnings by quantity or quality
of production."[37] Even where none of those defenses apply, the
agency can still resist an Equal Pay claim by showing that pay
differentials are based on some "factor other than sex."[38]

A 1992 case broadly analyzed that approach in assessing the
validity of different pay levels for custodians (all male) and
cleaners (all female) in a New York public school district. The
district court accepted the school board's claim that these differences reflected the civil service classification and examination
system, and found that system a "factor other than sex." But
the appeals court reversed.[39] Though federal courts had split
on this issue, the majority seem to concur with this circuit that
an employer like the school district must show more; in the
Equal Pay Act, Congress "rejected blanket assertions of facially
neutral job classification systems as valid factor-other-than-sex
defenses to EPA claims."[40] The school district thus had to demonstrate that its system "is rooted in legitimate business-related
differences in work responsibilities and qualifications for the
particular positions at issue."[41] It would also not do for an agency
or employer to base different pay levels on gender-specific job
labels like "custodian" and "cleaner."

**What remedies are available to a public employee who
proves a case of unlawful sex discrimination?**
As with race bias, a successful sex discrimination plaintiff is

entitled to be hired, rehired, or promoted and thus put where she or he would have been but for the unlawful action. Courts may also enjoin an unlawful policy or practice. Back pay is available to offset the effects of discrimination. Under Title VII, back pay may be recovered for two years prior to the filing of a claim with the EEOC or a suit in court. Under the Equal Pay Act, the normal limit on back pay is two years, though an additional year may be awarded if the employer's violation is found to have been "willful." Under Section 1983, the only limit on back pay as a remedy is the court's discretion.

One lingering remedial issue has recently been resolved by the Supreme Court. Title IX of the Education Amendments of 1972 specifically bars gender discrimination in all federally assisted educational programs. Though the most visible target of Title IX has been intercollegiate athletic programs, employment policies are also affected. But it remained unclear for two decades whether an individual plaintiff could recover damages. In *Franklin v. Gwinnett County Schools*,[42] the Supreme Court in 1992 finally resolved the issue in favor of a Title IX damage claim, thus adding one further remedy for the victim of unlawful sex or gender discrimination—a remedy that has no precise counterpart for the victim of racial bias.

**May courts order preferential or even quota hiring to remedy past discrimination?**

The issue may arise in two distinct ways. On one hand, courts occasionally order a government employer to undertake preferential hiring in order to remedy the effects of past discrimination. Title VII does not expressly authorize such remedies. In fact, some argue it shows a contrary intent since Section 703(j) declares that the Act should not be construed to require any employer to "grant preferential treatment to any individual or group . . . on account of any [racial] imbalance"[43] between the workforce and the local population or applicant pool. Nonetheless, some courts have found in Title VII the legal authority for limited use of race- or gender-conscious hiring orders. But the circumstances must be extreme. In cases involving mandated preference, the Supreme Court has recognized that judges may have to resort to race-conscious affirmative action when confronted with an employer or a labor union that has engaged in persistent or egregious discrimination, or where

such relief may be necessary to dissipate the lingering effects
of pervasive discrimination.[44] Later cases reflect several other
constraints in mandating affirmative action: Any persons hired
under such an order must be qualified; there must be proof
that less drastic means would fail to meet the need; and the
time period or the number of persons hired under the order
should normally be limited. Courts have been especially reluctant to extend such mandatory preference beyond the initial
hiring stage—for example, to promotion, where the effects on
already established nonminority workers may be unacceptable.

The more frequent battleground has become that of the
voluntary preferential program—affirmative action adopted by
an employer and challenged in court. Recent years have seen a
host of major cases, including several that reached the Supreme
Court involving both private and public employment. It
seemed clear from the start that the language quoted above
from Section 703(j) did not forbid employers from granting a
racial preference but simply revealed a congressional neutrality
on the issue. The earliest cases involved private employers and
the review of preferential hiring provisions in union agreements.

In 1987, the Court addressed similar issues in the public
employment setting, specifically an affirmative action plan of
the Santa Clara, California, Transportation Agency. The plan
authorized the agency to consider race or gender as a "plus
factor" in the hiring process. When a woman with a lower test
score was hired as the first female in a skilled craft position, a
man who had been rejected brought suit and the case eventually reached the Supreme Court. Speaking through Justice
Brennan, who had set the standards in the private employment
cases, the Court now approved the Santa Clara plan under
Title VII.[45] Such a plan, said the Court, must meet two strict
conditions: There must be a "manifest imbalance"[46] in the workforce with regard to the employment of women and minorities
in "traditionally segregated job categories";[47] and the plan must
not "unnecessarily trammel"[48] the interests of nonminority
workers.

This plan met both tests—the first because of the extreme
underrepresentation of women in the agency's skilled crafts;
and the second, because the plan's timing was limited to at-
taining (not maintaining) a balanced workforce, its hiring goals

were not to be construed as quotas, and no less favored male
employee had been denied a "legitimate firmly rooted expectation."[49] Justice O'Connor concurred on a narrower ground,
arguing that such cases should include statistically significant
evidence of a pattern or practice of excluding women or minorities from the workforce. She would therefore reject any plan
that sought to achieve racial or gender parity between the
agency's employment and the demography of the region.[50]
Three Justices dissented, believing the clear command of Title
VII was that race and gender may not be considered in employment actions—especially not in a case such as this one where
the agency had never actually practiced overt sex discrimination.

There has been one other major development affecting public employment. In a 1986 case involving provisions of a Michigan public school labor agreement,[51] the Court addressed race-
conscious layoff provisions that protected less senior minority
workers against reductions in force. Applying the Constitution's
Equal Protection Clause, the majority found the layoff plan
violative of the rights of nonminority teachers; unlike preference in initial hiring, "layoffs impose the entire burden of
achieving racial equality on particular individuals, often resulting in serious disruption of their lives."[52] Such a heavy
burden may not be imposed, in the absence of a court finding
that the remedial approach adopted by the school board was
essential. Such findings, which clearly had not been made in
this case, would among other things have to negate or refute
the efficacy of any less drastic remedies such as preferential or
race-conscious hiring programs.

The Supreme Court's most recent major case further compli-
cates the picture. Striking down Richmond's preferential pro-
curement program in 1989,[53] the Court revealed at least a
heightened standard of review of, if not a wholly new approach
to, voluntary governmental affirmative action programs. Justice
O'Connor, now writing for the Court, recognized that such a
plan barred some contractors from doing business with the city
solely on the basis of race and declared that nothing less than a
compelling interest would warrant such differential treatment.
The evidence the city had adduced to support its plan fell far
short, in the Court's view, of what was constitutionally required
to meet this new and strict test.

A government agency wishing to adopt such a preference must demonstrate past discrimination in the area to which the remedy applies, and not simply discrimination in the abstract or in other sectors. Thus in this case there should have been evidence comparing the percentage of minority contracts the city had awarded with the percentage of minority contractors in the area—and not simply comparing the contract allocation record with the minority population of the city. At the very least there should be evidence of past discrimination in the construction industry within the city.

There must also be such evidence with regard to any ethnic or other groups to whom the plan extended a preference; here it was fatal that the city offered no proof of past discrimination against nonblack minorities (e.g., Asians, Hispanics) who were also favored under the purchasing plan. Moreover, any such plan must be "narrowly tailored" to meet the effects of such past discrimination and thus could not (as the Richmond plan did) grant an absolute preference solely on the basis of race. Finally, an agency defending such a plan must show that less drastic remedies—for example, special recruitment or targeting of minority bidders, relaxation of procedures and bonding requirements, etc.—could not meet the need.

The dissenting justices insisted that the Equal Protection Clause did not limit the use of racial classifications to those that remedy past wrongs.[54] They pointed out the poignant dilemma a governmental body or agency would face if the only way it could defend or justify its use of a racial or gender preference was by admitting to having practiced unlawful race or sex discrimination in the past. Rather than looking only to the past, they urged the Court to continue to analyze the probable future impact of such race- or gender-conscious plans and sustain them on that basis.

It is not yet clear how far the *Croson* (Richmond) case extends beyond purchasing—and specifically, to public employment. The Supreme Court soon took a rather different view in sustaining affirmative action requirements that had been imposed on broadcast licensees.[55] Several lower courts have distinguished *Croson* in continuing to uphold preferential employment programs. For example, a federal court has upheld a comprehensive Birmingham, Alabama, affirmative action plan that includes numerical hiring goals.[56] Other courts have upheld a Detroit police plan that ensures one black patrolman will be promoted for every white officer promoted at the same level,[57] and a race-conscious teacher transfer plan of the Cincinnati public schools.[58] Federal courts in these cases found that both the goals and the means of such preferential policies survived the *Croson* decision and were consistent with the Supreme Court's earlier cases dealing with affirmative action in public employment. And perhaps most significant, the Supreme Court itself declined in the spring of 1992—three years after *Croson*—to upset a race-conscious preferential hiring plan recently developed by the city of Philadelphia to achieve greater balance in the makeup of its police force.[59] While routine denials of review never officially imply a judgment on the merits, the Court's refusal to revisit this highly volatile and visible area in the post-*Croson* period affords at least small solace to advocates of affirmative action programs and policies in public employment.

### What rights are enjoyed by disabled and handicapped public employees?

Since 1973, the Rehabilitation Act[60] has conferred substantial protection on state and local employees of agencies that receive federal funds. In 1978 the provisions of this Act were extended to federal employees. (In the summer of 1992 the Americans with Disabilities Act for the first time extended similar federal protection to most workers in the private sector.)

The Rehabilitation Act requires any covered agency or department to develop and file a plan providing for the hiring, placement, and advancement of persons with disabilities. The Act then sets forth a basic standard of protection: No otherwise qualified person with handicaps "shall, solely by reason of his or her handicap, be denied the benefits of, or be subjected to discrimination" in or under any federal or federally assisted program.[61] The Act defines a handicapped individual as one who (1) has a physical or mental impairment that substantially limits one or more of such person's life activities, (2) has a record of such an impairment, or (3) is regarded as having such an impairment.[62] The definitions evoke obvious examples of handicapped persons—those whose physical mobility or hearing or eyesight is impaired. This test has been applied increasingly to less obvious forms of handicap, as in the case of a federal attorney who was held to have been wrongfully discharged on the basis of drug use (and arrests therefor), since he had completed a rehabilitation program and was otherwise qualified.[63] Persons who carry certain contagious diseases have also been held to be handicapped and are thus within the Act's protections.

Once a person is determined to be handicapped, an employer's decision to hire, discharge, or not to promote that person must under the Rehabilitation Act be justified by factors other than the handicap. Otherwise such an adverse action constitutes discrimination in violation of Section 504 of the Act. Discrimination against disabled or handicapped persons may of course be proved by direct evidence. But evidence of disparate impact may also serve to establish discrimination by indirect means.

The procedure for pursuing discrimination claims under the Rehabilitation Act is substantially the same as that for race and gender-bias cases, described earlier in this chapter. But the central issues in a handicap discrimination case are likely to be different. One critical issue in this field is the explicit requirement that a person be "otherwise qualified." This phrase denotes a person who is able to meet all of a program's requirements in spite of the handicap. The Supreme Court has focused on the applicant's ability to perform the job "without a reasonable probability of substantial injury to herself or others."[64]

If an applicant is presently qualified to perform the job, then a refusal to employ that person would represent unlawful discrimination on the basis of handicap. But such a straightforward case is relatively rare. If the applicant is not so clearly qualified, accommodation may be required of the agency. The duty to accommodate has been defined in general terms: While an employer need not be required to make "fundamental" or "substantial" modifications to accommodate the handicapped, it may be required to make "reasonable" ones.[65] This standard has been further refined by the lower courts in asking whether "reasonable accommodation can be made, without undue hardship to the employer, sufficient to enable the applicant to perform the essential requirements of the job" without a reasonable risk of injury to self or others. Then the ultimate issue becomes how extensive those accommodations need be, a matter on which a number of courts have spoken.

One court recently declared, for example, that a federal computer operator with multiple sclerosis would be entitled to an arrangement enabling her to work at home, unless the agency could demonstrate the requisite "undue hardship."[66] That standard would not be met, said the court, simply by noting the often short deadlines in the agency's operations, or the values of frequent face-to-face contact.[67]

Sometimes the accommodation issue will be keenly disputed. A government agency as employer has the burden in such cases "to gather sufficient information from the applicant and qualified experts to determine what accommodations are necessary to enable the applicant to perform the job safely." If the necessary accommodation is not reasonable, or if no accommodation at all can be made because of a mismatch between the handicap and the job, a denial of employment would not violate the Rehabilitation Act. Yet the applicant still has one last chance to present rebuttal evidence, for example, with regard to forms of accommodation that the agency may have rejected or may not even have considered.

## NOTES

1. Pub. L. No. 102–166, 105 Stat. 1071 (1991).
2. *Franklin v. Gwinnett County Public Schools*, 117 L. Ed. 2d 208 (1992).
3. 42 U.S.C. § 1981 (1988).
4. 42 U.S.C. § 1983 (1988).
5. 42 U.S.C. § 2000e (1988).
6. 42 U.S.C. § 2000e–16 (1988).
7. *Brown v. General Services Administration*, 425 U.S. 820 (1976).
8. 2 U.S.C. §§ 1201–1224 (West Supp. 1992).
9. 2 U.S.C. § 1220 (West Supp. 1992).
10. *McDonald v. Santa Fe Trail Transportation Co.*, 427 U.S. 273 (1976).
11. *See* New York Times, June 19, 1992, at B1, cols. 2–5.
12. 42 U.S.C.A. § 1981(b) (West Supp. 1992).
13. *E.g.*, *Griggs v. Duke Power Co.*, 401 U.S. 424 (1971).
14. 42 U.S.C.A. § 2000e–2(1) (West Supp. 1992).
15. 42 U.S.C.A. § 1981a(c) (West Supp. 1992).
16. *Vulcan Society of New York City Fire Department v. Civil Service Commission*, 490 F.2d 387 (2d Cir. 1973).
17. 401 U.S. at 431. (1971).

18.  401 U.S. at 433.

19.  29 C.F.R. § 1607 (1991).

20.  *Wards Cove Packing Co. v. Atonio*, 490 U.S. 642 (1989).

21.  42 U.S.C.A. § 2000e–2(k) (West Supp. 1992).

22.  *Price Waterhouse v. Hopkins*, 490 U.S. 228 (1989).

23.  *Howard v. Lockheed-Georgia Co.*, 372 F. Supp. 854 (N.D. Ga. 1974).

24.  42 U.S.C.A. § 1981a(b)(1) (West Supp. 1992).

25.  42 U.S.C. § 2000e (1988).

26.  42 U.S.C. § 2000e–2(e) (1988).

27.  29 U.S.C. §§ 201 *et seq.* (1988).

28.  42 U.S.C. § 2000e(1) (1988).

29.  *General Electric Co. v. Gilbert*, 429 U.S. 125 (1976); *Geduldig v. Aiello*, 417 U.S. 484 (1974); *Frontiero v. Richardson*, 411 U.S. 677 (1973); *Reed v. Reed*, 404 U.S. 71 (1971).

30.  *Craig v. Boren*, 429 U.S. 190 (1976).

31.  433 U.S. 321 (1977).

32.  *United Automobile Workers Union v. Johnson Controls, Inc.*, 113 L. Ed. 2d 158 (1991).

33.  *Hughes v. Lipscher*, 720 F. Supp. 454 (D.N.J. 1989), *vacated and remanded*, 906 F.2d 961 (3d Cir. 1990).

34.  *Keckstein v. Independent School District*, 509 F.2d 1062 (8th Cir. 1975).

35.  *Cleveland Board of Education v. LaFleur*, 414 U.S. 632 (1974).

36.  *Dothard v. Rawlinson*, 432 U.S. 321 (1977).

37.  29 U.S.C. § 206(d)(1) (1988).

38.  29 U.S.C. § 206(d)(1)(iv) (1988).

39.  *Aldrich v. Randolph Central School District*, 963 F.2d 520 (2d Cir. 1992).

40.  963 F.2d at 525.

41.  963 F.2d at 525.

42.  117 L. Ed. 2d 208 (1992).

43.  42 U.S.C. § 2000e–2(j) (1988).

44.  *See, e.g., Local 28, Sheet Metal Workers Int'l Ass'n v. EEOC*, 478 U.S. 421 (1986).

45.  *Johnson v. Transportation Agency, Santa Clara County*, 480 U.S. 616, 666 (1987).

46.  *Id.* at 632.

47.  *Id.*

48.  *Id.* at 637–40.

49.  *Id.* at 638.

50.  *Id.* at 637–42.

51.  *Wygant v. Jackson Board of Education*, 476 U.S. 267 (1986).

52.  *Id.* at 283.

53. *Richmond, Virginia v. J. A. Croson Co.*, 488 U.S. 469 (1989).
54. *Id.* at U.S. at 555–56.
55. *Metro Boradcasting v. FCC*, 111 L. Ed. 2d 445 (1990).
56. New York Times, Aug. 18, 1992, at A12, cols. 5–6.
57. *Detroit Police Officers Association v. Young*, 765 F. Supp. 393 (E.D. Mich. 1991).
58. *Jacobson v. Cincinnati Board of Education*, 961 F.2d 100 (6th Cir. 1992).
59. *Fraternal Order of Police Lodge No. 5 v. City of Phiuladelphia*, 118 L. Ed. 2d 389 (1992).
60. 29 U.S.C. §§ 701–796 (1988).
61. 29 U.S.C. § 794 (1988).
62. 29 U.S.C. § 706(7)(B) (1988).
63. *Nisperos v. Acting Commissioner*, 720 F. Supp. 1424 (N.D. Cal. 1989).
64. *School Board v. Arline*, 480 U.S. 273 (2987).
65. *See* 480 U.S. at 287–88 & n.17.
66. *Langon v. Department of Health and Human Services*, 959 F. Supp. 1053 (D.D.C. 1992).
67. *Id.* at 1060.

# VII

# Procedural Rights of Public Employees

Opportunities may be denied in many different ways to public employees or people seeking public positions. An applicant may simply be rejected or denied employment. Once hired, a government worker may be dismissed or discharged. Where the expectation is that an employee will move "up or out" after a probationary period, denial of tenure or permanent job status amounts to a discharge. One who holds a term or limited appointment may simply be denied renewal or reappointment. When budgets or agency needs shrink, there may be layoffs with no firm commitment to rehire. Positions are sometimes phased out or eliminated or may be so drastically changed that incumbents are effectively displaced. Short of complete loss of employment, government workers may suffer salary freezes, suspensions, demotions, and other less drastic sanctions.

At this point procedures become crucial. In all these situations, the affected government employee needs to know how he or she can protect his or her employment status. And however strong may be the substantive claim or legal interest, it is of little value to the individual employee without channels of redress—channels that call the agency to account and offer a forum where competing claims may be tested before an impartial decision maker. If, for example, a public worker may be fired without a hearing, then abstract principles of free speech or equality or privacy may have little value.

The importance of some sort of hearing cannot be exaggerated. Even an employee who can afford to file a lawsuit and bear the other risks and burdens of litigation may face insurmountable odds if the agency need not provide an internal hearing or formal review before taking an adverse personnel action. Without such procedures, the reasons for the adverse action may be obscure or even nonexistent, leaving the employee tilting an illusory windmills.

The values of an agency hearing are several. Not only may it be essential to vindicating the rights and interests of the individual employee. The whole system works far better if disputes can be resolved within the agency and kept from getting to already crowded courts. Hearings also serve to keep agencies honest in ways that are important to the lawmakers who create, empower, and fund those agencies. The agency may also be helped in shaping its own rules and procedures by the hearing process and its results.

Finally, the confidence of public workers in the fairness of particular agencies, and government in general, may depend considerably on the procedures available to review adverse actions and sanctions. For all these reasons, as well as the basic need to protect the legal rights of individual employees, a hearing system is essential.

## Does the law guarantee a hearing to a discharged public employee?

Roughly half of all government workers are covered by civil service systems. Most civil service laws provide for some form of hearing in connection with a discharge or dismissal—though the timing and adequacy of that hearing may vary. In the federal civil service, which covers 85 percent of all federal workers, the hearing requirement is of long standing. Nearly a century ago, in 1897, President William McKinley issued an executive order that guaranteed that no civil servant would be removed "except for just cause and upon written charges of which the accused shall have full notice and an opportunity to make defense."[1] Those provisions were codified in the Lloyd-La Follette Act of 1912,[2] which governed federal civil service procedures until the adoption in 1978 of the Civil Service Reform Act.[3]

The Civil Service Reform Act (CSRA) was the first major overhaul of civil service laws since the establishment of the system in 1883 and created what the Supreme Court has called "an elaborate new comprehensive scheme that encompasses substantive provisions forbidding arbitrary action by [federal employers]."[4] It reflects what one commentator has called "the unification of decades of piecemeal efforts to afford protection to federal employees from wrongful or arbitrary action by their employer and gives agencies clear guidelines regarding employment termination standards."[5]

In part the CSRA expands the rights of federal employees to organize collectively (a subject treated in chapter IV) and creates the Federal Labor Relations authority as a public sector counterpart to the National Labor Relations Board.[6] The law also creates the Merit Systems Protection Board, a new agency that has no private sector counterpart but is charged with safeguarding the rights of federal workers.[7] The Act requires all federal agencies to establish performance appraisal standards that define objective criteria by which employees' work is measured.[8] Agencies may then take adverse action (defined as removal, suspension for more than fourteen days, reduction in grade, reduction in pay or furlough for thirty days or less) either for "unacceptable performance" or "to promote the efficiency of the service."[9]

Removal and demotion, the ultimate sanctions, are sparingly invoked. During fiscal year 1990, of well more than a million and a half covered federal employees, only 370 were removed and 128 were demoted for poor performance.[10] In those few cases, however, the procedures are now made clear by the Reform Act: the employee is entitled to (1) thirty days advance written notice of the proposed action, identifying specific instances of unacceptable performance on which the action is based, and the critical elements of the employee's position to which those standards apply; (2) the right to be represented by an attorney; (3) a reasonable time in which to answer orally and in writing; and (4) a written decision.[11]

At the less severe end of the scale, an employee suspended for fourteen days or less for such cause "as will promote the efficiency of the service" is also entitled to advance written notice stating the specific reasons for the action; a reasonable time in which to respond orally and in writing; the right to be represented by counsel; and a written decision with specific reasons.[12] Graver sanctions based on the "efficiency of the service," rather than "unacceptable performance," are governed by similar sanctions, including thirty days notice of the proposed action and not less than seven days in which to respond.[13]

The agency has in each case the option of providing a hearing in lieu of, or in addition to, the employer's chance to respond. The employee who wishes to appeal or seek review of an adverse decision at the agency level may either pursue arbitration under a collective bargaining agreement (if the matter is covered under the agreement) or may seek a hearing before the Merit Systems Protection Board or an administrative law judge, at which the employee may be represented by an attorney or other advocate.[14]

The board will normally sustain the agency action, unless it finds that action not supported by substantial evidence or by a preponderance of the evidence, though the employee may also prevail by showing that the agency committed "harmful error" in applying its procedures, or that the decision reflected a discriminatory personnel practice, or that it was otherwise not in accordance with law. An adverse judgment of the board may be further appealed to the United States Court of Appeals for the Federal Circuit, which will set aside the board's decision if it is found to be "(1) arbitrary, capricious, an abuse of discretion or otherwise not in accordance with law; or (2) obtained without procedures required by law, rule or regulation having been followed; or (3) unsupported by substantial evidence."[15]

When the decision has gone in an employee's favor, it may be appealed to the court only upon motion of the Office of Personnel Management and will be reversed only if the board has erred in interpreting a law or regulation in a way that will have "substantial impact" on the federal personnel system. This relatively new and uniform system replaced nearly a century of patchwork policy and practice that varied substantially from one agency to another and left substantial confusion and uncertainty among federal workers. It is probably still too soon to know how well the new approach of the Civil Service Reform Act has succeeded in enhancing fairness, uniformity and agency accountability—all vital goals of a rational and humane national personnel system.

## Does the Constitution guarantee a hearing where statute or regulation does not?

The answer to this question is complex, confusing, and evolving. Since the mid 1960s, courts have held that many types of government benefits may not be revoked or removed without a prior hearing. A welfare or unemployment compensation recipient may not be taken off the rolls;[16] a state college or university student may not be expelled;[17] a driver's license or parole may not be revoked,[18] or other benefits terminated, without some sort of hearing.[19] But the Supreme Court has stopped short of ensuring such rights for public employees. Until recently, in fact, it was widely assumed that government employees had only those procedural protections given them by statute, regulation, or bargaining agreement.

Recent years have brought the emergence of a limited and qualified public employee's claim to a hearing. A pair of 1972 cases applied to procedural claims a doctrine that had already been used to protect substantive interests of the public worker—the doctrine that public employment was no longer a mere "privilege" that government could withdraw, or condition, on any grounds it wished. But the Court declined to hold that all agency terminations required due process. In *Board of Regents v. Roth*,[20] the justices held that the simple, routine denial of reappointment or the refusal to extend a year-to-year contract of public employment still did not require a hearing. The conditions conducive to a claim of due process seem to be three: when the dismissal abridged an independent constitutional right, such as freedom of speech; when the dismissal violated the employee's "property" rights; or when the government worker's constitutional interest in "liberty" was violated by an agency action. Otherwise, a public employee could be denied continuing employment without a hearing. Thus the procedural protections available to a public employee remained narrower and more limited than those enjoyed by almost any other government beneficiary.

**Does an action that abridges substantive constitutional rights require a hearing?**

Yes. In the other 1972 case, *Perry v. Sindermann*,[21] the Court reaffirmed that government may not fire a person for asserting freedom of speech or some other similarly fundamental interest. Even where the speech or other protected activity may not have been cited as the basis for the action, allegations of free speech abridgment by a state college professor who had been denied reappointment after taking part in a protected activity "plainly . . . present a constitutional claim [since] a teacher's public criticism of his superiors on matters of public concern may be constitutionally protected and may, therefore, be an impermissible basis for termination of his employment."[22] Thus close proximity between speech and adverse action, as well as direct attribution, may be sufficient to trigger this interest.

**When does the abridgment of a public employee's "property" right require a hearing?**

In the *Roth* and *Sindermann* cases, the Supreme Court established that a hearing was required where an employee could show a "property" interest in continued employment. That interest was to be defined by state law and required proof of a "legitimate claim of entitlement" to the job.[23] Thus a strong personal desire to continue in the job, or the absence of ready alternatives, would not suffice to establish a "property" interest. The holding of formal tenure would, however, clearly trigger a "property" claim. Even where tenure was not guaranteed by written contract, a public employee "might be able to show from the circumstances of his service—and from other relevant facts—that he has a legitimate claim of entitlement to job tenure."[24] Thus proof of "de facto tenure" derived from long-standing policy might necessitate a hearing. Quite clearly, the dismissal of even a nontenured employee during the term of a contract requires a hearing, since the employee has a "property" interest in maintaining employment through that term.[25]

On the other hand, persons with so-called permanent jobs do not always have a "property" interest. Four years after the initial cases, the Supreme Court elaborated in *Bishop v. Wood*,[26] a case involving the discharge of a North Carolina police officer whose position was described as "permanent" after three years on the job. While the state laws could fairly be read as conferring a "property" interest, they were ambiguous. The federal district judge, presumably quite familiar with state law, had ruled the officer "held his position at will and the pleasure of the city."[27] The High Court accepted that view and held that a "property" interest did not exist. That judgment substantially qualified the scope of the *Roth* and *Sindermann* cases four years earlier.

Then in 1985 the Supreme Court offered a more favorable view of "property" interests in *Cleveland Board of Education v. Loudermill*,[28] a case involving the discharge of an Ohio public school security guard for allegedly making false statements on his application form. Ohio state law made him a "classified civil service employee" and entitled him to retain his position "during good behavior and efficient service."[29] He could be dismissed under state law only for "misfeasance, malfeasance or nonfeasance in office." The federal district judge found no "property" interest in such language. But the court of appeals reversed, holding that an Ohio employee had a reasonable expectation of continued employment and thus a "property" interest sufficient to claim a hearing.[30]

The Supreme Court agreed that a "property" interest was present. For a majority of the justices, the "private interest in retaining employment"[31] and the "opportunity for the employee to present his side of the case"[32] outweighed the "governmental interest in immediate termination."[33] Even though the same state law that created the expectation of continued employment also limited the procedures by which an employee might assert that interest—a nexus the Supreme Court had earlier found persuasive—the Court now insisted that the procedures must on their own meet constitutional due process standards.

The state could not, said the Court, in effect give with one hand and then take away with the other: "[I]t is settled that the 'bitter with the sweet' approach misconceives the constitutional guarantee."[34] (The justices went on to consider the related question of timing—whether the hearing must precede termination; we address this issue in a later section of this chapter.)

The lower courts have recently applied the *Loudermill* standards in ways that enhance the public employee's "property" interest. A later Ohio federal case granted hearing rights to a police officer who had been discharged without a hearing after he made critical statements about the city administration. There, as in *Loudermill* itself, the Ohio state laws created a sufficient expectation of continued employment to generate the requisite "property" interest.[35] Another federal appeals court recently found a "property" claim in state laws that assured a deputy sheriff his employment would continue during "good behavior and satisfactory performance of duties."[36]

## Can an employee claim a "property" interest through long time service alone?

Only if the term is very long, and even then the claim is doubtful. Several courts have held that satisfactory service, without tenure, for six or eight years would not alone create a "property" interest. One case that seemed to reach a different conclusion involved a teacher who had taught for twenty-nine years and was suddenly dismissed without a hearing. The court of appeals held that such a person should at least be given a chance to show that such a period of satisfactory teaching created a "property" interest.[37] But such a bare length-of-service

claim seems problematic in light of the Supreme Court's holding in the *Bishop* case that even public workers whose appoint-
ments are labeled "permanent" may not be able to assert such
a hearing right.

### Does the abridgment of a public employee's "liberty" inter-est give rise to a hearing right?

Yes. The Supreme Court held in the *Roth* and *Sindermann*
cases that a termination might deprive a public employee of
"liberty" in two relevant ways: Such an action might "seriously
damage [the employee's] standing and associations in the community," or it might impose "a stigma or other disability that
foreclosed his freedom to take advantage of other employment
opportunities."[38] Under this standard, a discharged employee
could establish a "liberty" interest through either "the objective
consideration of employment deprivation [or] subjective consideration of social stigma." But the routine, unexplained denial
of continuing employment would not give rise to a "liberty"-
based hearing any more readily than it would generate a "property" interest.[39]

Later cases indicated that in fact a quite substantial deprivation is required for such a "liberty" claim. Courts have held,
for example, that terminations based on the following charges
do not meet this standard: "malfeasance," noncooperation, display of "anti-establishment obsession," failure to perform a
particular task, failure to meet certain minimum-standard requirements, or failure to cooperate with fellow workers.[40] On
the other hand, courts have found the following charges to
require a hearing because they abridged an employee's "liberty" interest: alleged racism, dishonesty and lack of integrity,
alleged mental instability, lack of performance, unwillingness
to carry out institutional policies, and moral turpitude.[41] As the
article analyzing these contrasting cases noted, "the distinction
seems less than clear."[42]

One recent federal case involving the discharge of an Idaho
teacher for alcohol abuse suggested that a "liberty" interest is
likeliest to be found when either the employee's good name,
reputation, honor, or integrity is disparaged by charges such
as immorality, dishonesty, alcoholism or political subversion;
or when the state imposes a stigma that reduces other employment opportunities.[43] The latter standard demands more than

simply reduced earning capacity or diminished prestige; permanent exclusion from, or at least serious interruption of, employment seems to be the essential catalyst.

In deciding whether a "liberty" interest is implicated, courts take note of such factors as the level of the position, the employee's age, and the financial impact of the discharge. A court might also consider the degree to which the employee has private sector alternatives if public employment is foreclosed. Yet the definition of the "liberty" basis for a hearing lacks the clarity that surrounds the "property" claim, and it continues to require case-by-case analysis.

The Supreme Court has added two important qualifications in later cases. In 1977 the justices held that a "liberty" interest leading to a hearing could be lost or jeopardized if the employee did not claim it by challenging the truth of the allegedly stigmatizing statements. The purpose of a hearing in such a case, said the Court, "is solely 'to provide the person an opportunity to clear his name.' " The Court then added this explanation: "If he does not challenge the substantial truth of the material in question, no hearing would afford a promise of achieving that result for him."[44]

Then in a 1991 case, the Supreme Court further qualified the "liberty" claim.[45] A clinical psychologist named Siegert resigned his position at a federal hospital after being notified he was about to be fired for various shortcomings. When he applied for another federal post and sought recommendations, his former supervisor described him as "inept and unethical, perhaps the least trustworthy individual I have supervised in my thirteen years." After the new job was denied, on the basis of this assessment, the psychologist brought suit, seeking a hearing on the charges. The Supreme Court eventually rejected the claim. Though recognizing the harm such statements could do to an employee's reputation and job prospects, the majority held those charges nonetheless failed to create a "liberty" interest because they had not been made in the course of the termination itself but only after the employee had left the position to which they referred.[46] To one of the dissenting justices, the majority view "suggests that reputational injury deprives a person of liberty only when combined with a loss of employment, not future employment."[47]

**Must the charge be communicated to others in order to deprive the employee of "liberty"?**

Yes, said the Supreme Court in its 1976 decision in *Bishop v. Wood*.[48] The discharged police officer, having lost on his property claim, also advanced a "liberty" interest—both because the charges given him by the city manager created a stigma, he argued, and because those charges were false. The Supreme Court was willing to assume the charges were indeed false, but held that fact by itself did not violate the officer's protected interest in "liberty." The other contention was more difficult. The city manager had told the officer he was being terminated for failure to follow certain orders, for poor attendance at police training classes, for impairing morale within the department, and for other conduct unbecoming an officer.

None of these charges had been communicated to anyone else at the time of the discharge. They became public only when they were written down in the course of preparing for the trial of the lawsuit. The Supreme Court held that no matter how serious, or how erroneous, the charges might be, they could not trigger a "liberty" interest (and thus a due process claim) unless they had been conveyed to others.[49] As with a claim of libel or slander, "liberty" presupposed a stigma that could not arise when the charges remained private between the employer and employee, with no knowledge by third parties. The officer's claim might have been stronger if, before bringing suit, he had sought another job and the charges had been conveyed to a prospective employer; even under the Supreme Court's *Siegert* ruling, such charges would have been part of the termination process, even though not made public until later.

In this vein, a federal court of appeals recently held that a Florida police department violated a discharged officer's "liberty" interest when it placed in public records some stigmatizing information about the officer's conduct. The information became accessible to the public, as state law required, at the conclusion of the inquiry that led to the termination. That was enough for the appeals court: "The file and report have stigmatized [the officer] in the eyes of potential law enforcement employers and in the minds of citizens reviewing this public information."[50] Thus the agency need not have broadcast the charges to the world; a "liberty"-creating stigma can occur through the relatively passive dissemination a public file involves.

### Can a "liberty" interest arise if no reason at all is given for a termination?

Such a claim would be difficult to prove. The applicable statute might conceivably provide that an employee could be fired only on specific grounds that, if they were made explicit, would be clearly stigmatizing. Thus if an employee were discharged without a hearing under that law, the only inference that others could draw would be the commission of one or more of the specific and stigmatizing acts. Here the employee might be able to show that the mere discharge, without reasons being given, was either in complete violation of the statute or, if in compliance with that law, reflected a charge that could not help but damage reputation or professional standing and prospects. But such a situation would be rare.

The Supreme Court has addressed a related issue in a way that may offer modest help to public employees facing unexplained adverse actions.[51] In 1977, the Court ruled that when constitutionally protected conduct (such as free speech) played a substantial part in a public employee's discharge, the trial judge must determine whether the employer would have reached the same result in the absence of the protected conduct.[52] That ruling has limited value here, since it requires proof not only of at least one factor in the termination but proof specifically of the constitutionally protected nature of that conduct. The victim of a wholly unexplained termination would be hard put to meet that standard.

There is one other possible recourse. The Supreme Court suggested in the *Roth* case that an unexplained termination might create a "liberty" interest if it severely curtailed other employment opportunities. Such a situation might arise if, for example, dismissal of a professor from one state university made him unemployable at all other public universities within the state. The Court noted that where a termination, with or without reasons, "foreclose[d] a range of opportunities,"[53] a due process claim might arise. On the other hand, the Court deemed insufficient a claim that a teacher would simply become "somewhat less attractive to other employers" after an unexplained denial of reappointment.[54]

### How much "process" is "due" when a hearing is required?

The Supreme Court has never fully detailed the ingredients, though it has several times addressed the issue. Each case must balance the conflicting claims of the employee seeking redress and the government agency's need to act efficiently and decisively in major personnel matters. To the extent any pattern emerges, the hearing would usually involve, at the very least, notice of the charges and an opportunity to respond within a reasonable time, orally or in writing or both. Some courts would permit the employee to introduce evidence in his or her own behalf and to cross-examine accusers.

That process might require the aid of retained counsel, if the employee can afford it, though due process does not force the agency to provide counsel at public expense. The decision maker should be impartial and unbiased, should have the authority to order relief that would meet the employee's needs, and should provide the employee with at least a summary of findings and conclusions. Then there should be some avenue of further appeal, sometimes within the agency or government and eventually to a court if the employee wishes to press the claim. These are the elements of due process most often cited by courts that find a hearing to be required.[55]

### Does the discharged public employee have a right to an impartial or unbiased hearing?

Yes, at least in principle. Impartiality in the hearing panel or officer is obviously of profound importance for public employees. The problem is one of establishing when a decision maker is biased to a degree that denies due process. The Supreme Court held in 1976 that a school board could impartially review the dismissal of several teachers who had engaged in an illegal strike against that board.[56] The board's proximity to the issues posed no risk of inherent bias or conflict of interest, said the High Court. Nor did the fact that its members were familiar with the issues leading to the dismissal serve to "disqualify a decision-maker."

The force of this judgment may be tempered by several

factors—the clear illegality of the strike, the explicit authority given the board under state law to act as it had acted, and the absence of another appropriate hearing body. (Even the state supreme court, which found the school board to have been fatally biased, could only suggest that it should have rendered an initial decision subject to state court review.) The issue of impartiality and bias was presented again in the *Loudermill* case, though the Supreme Court majority did not reach it.

Meanwhile, a number of lower courts have recently addressed claims of procedural bias. Though the rulings are not in complete accord, these cases have shown sympathy for the employee who may have suffered from bias or prejudgment. One such case sustained a California teacher's claim that the school board denied him due process when the only hearing it held took place after the board had reached a decision to terminate.[57] Another federal appeals court found due process lacking when public statements the decision maker had made before the hearing seriously undermined his claim of impartiality.[58] Other federal appeals courts have found a denial of due process, either in evidence of the hearing officer's personal animosity toward the employee or in the direct personal involvement of agency members in the termination process that the hearing later challenged.[59] Meanwhile, another federal circuit found a posttermination hearing sufficient to "ferret out bias, pretext, deception and corruption by the employer in discharging the employee," even though the pretermination hearing was almost certainly tainted to a constitutionally significant degree.[60]

Thus the pattern presented by the cases remains mixed. Absence of bias is surely an essential element of due process, as the Supreme Court has repeatedly insisted in other contexts. But proof of disabling bias in public employee discharge cases remains difficult, and the precise standards remain elusive.

## Must a hearing occur before termination to satisfy due process?

The timing of a hearing may be crucial. In few situations is there clearer application of the adage, "justice delayed is justice denied." Thus it is vital to know not only whether but when a public employee facing dismissal may contest the basis of the agency action. The Supreme Court's approach to the issue has been uncertain and confusing, though some clarity has recently emerged. In 1974, the Court was split three ways: some justices argued that all public employees were entitled to a pretermination hearing; others felt such a hearing was never required; and those in the middle insisted on balancing in each case the individual's and governmental interests.

The majority in *Arnett v. Kennedy* sustained the constitutionality of the federal Lloyd-La Follette Act, which afforded only an informal appeal prior to termination and guaranteed a trial-type hearing only after the agency action took effect.[61]

The High Court revisited the issue in the 1985 *Loudermill* case involving the Ohio civil servants.[62] Once again the justices were split three ways, with a moderate majority in the middle. After finding these employees had a sufficient "property" interest under state law to claim a hearing of some type, the Court then addressed the issue of timing. A balancing of individual and governmental needs led the majority to conclude that all factors called for some procedure prior to termination. From the employees' perspective, "the private interest in retaining employment cannot be gainsaid."[63] Though the agency argued it must be able to proceed with dispatch, the justices insisted that "affording an employee an opportunity to respond prior to termination would impose neither a significant administrative burden nor intolerable delays."[64] In fact, the agency "shares the employee's interest in avoiding disruption and erroneous decisions."[65] During the challenge, the employer should recognize that "it is preferable to keep a qualified employee on than to train a new one."[66] And if the agency "perceives a significant hazard in keeping the employee on the job, it can avoid the problem by suspending with pay."[67] Thus on all counts, due process and the balancing of contending interests required at least an "opportunity to respond prior to termination."[68]

That opportunity did not, however, demand a full dress hearing. In fact, the employees in the *Loudermill* case had asked only "notice and an opportunity to respond"[69]—and that was all the Court was prepared to give them. "The opportunity to present reasons, either in person or in writing, why proposed action should not be taken,"[70] the Court explained, "is a fundamental due process requirement."[71] One wonders whether discharged employees who sought a fuller hearing would have fared better than did the *Loudermill* plaintiffs. But there is clear evidence the Court was not inclined to go further: "To require more than this prior to termination would intrude to an unwarranted extent on the government's interest in quickly removing an unsatisfactory employee."[72]

The Court's refusal to order a full adversarial hearing before termination reflects several factors. One was Ohio's provision for a "full post-termination hearing," even though such a hearing might occur long after the firing. In one of these cases, in fact, it took nine months—a delay the Court found consistent with due process, though noting that "at some point, a delay in the post-termination hearing would become a constitutional violation."[73]

The most the Court would say of the posttermination appeal is that it must occur "at a meaningful time"[74]—a standard the dissenters felt might have been breached in this case.[75] Though it is not clear how long a delay would be excessive in the majority's view, the nine months involved here fell within the ambit of due process. This factor, like most others in the issue of timing, depends on the circumstances and the balancing of agency and employee interests.

All that can be said with confidence is that the informality of the required pretermination procedure must be weighed against the adequacy of the posttermination hearing or appeal— and that includes how soon such process is available. It may also include the issue of remedies and, specifically, whether a discharged employee who eventually prevails is reinstated with back pay and other retroactive benefits. Making the vindicated employee whole in this way is no substitute for due process denied but does at least make protracted redress more palatable.

### Do the guarantees of due process apply to agency action short of dismissal?

Some laws and agency rules address the nature of the sanction to which procedural rights apply, as with the new federal civil service provisions reviewed earlier in this chapter. Where that is not the case, the answer depends both on the nature of the sanctions and other circumstances. A forced resignation may, for example, have exactly the same effect and may give rise to similar procedural rights.[76] On the other hand, many milder sanctions will not trigger the full range of due process rights. The Supreme Court has not directly addressed this issue. A 1973 case involving a public employee suspension was sent back to the lower courts for reconsideration,[77] and a similar case was argued before the Court three years later but was remanded after the agency revised its rules to require presuspension hearings.[78]

Meanwhile, the lower courts have proceeded on their own. In cases involving suspension, even for fairly short periods, public employees have usually been held entitled to a hearing, sometimes even before suspension.[79] In the *Loudermill* case, the Supreme Court assumed that if the agency felt it must suspend an employee before dismissal, such action would be "with pay"—suggesting that other types of suspensions should be treated like dismissals. Other kinds of lesser sanctions, even some kinds of lateral transfers, have been held to require some sort of hearing where a "property" or "liberty" interest is infringed.[80] An adverse job evaluation, which did not cause loss of employment but diminished the prospects for advancement, has also been found to require a hearing.[81]

On the other hand, there are cases in which fairly substantial sanctions—demotions in rank or grade or denial of a security clearance—have been sustained without formal procedures. Given the range of possible sanctions short of termination or dismissal, generalizations in this area are risky. Here as with other procedural matters, courts are likely to continue to balance individual and governmental interests.

### Is a hearing ever available to a rejected applicant for public employment?

Only under most unusual conditions, unless the applicable law so provides. Clearly an applicant has no "property" interest in a job that has not yet been offered, much less held. There may in a few situations be a "liberty" interest sufficient to generate such a claim. In one case, an applicant for a clerical position was turned down because of "unsatisfactory references." When the issue got to court, the judge ruled that due process entitled the applicant to know the sources and the substance of the allegedly damaging references and to have an opportunity to refute the charges. "All persons," said the court, "including [the applicant] should have a right to or interest in fair consideration for placement on the eligible civil service list."[82] But the situations under which such a claim would be heard are few and far between. Applicants, for the most part, have only such procedural rights as statutes may confer.

### Are some positions in the public service "above" or "beyond" due process?

There are certain situations to which due process claims may not apply. In 1988, a unanimous Supreme Court sustained the discharge of a suspected homosexual from a highly sensitive position in the National Security Agency.[83] The employee claimed that any termination must follow an Act of Congress that required pretermination hearings even for NSA positions. But the agency argued, and the justices agreed without dissent, that Congress had not meant to repeal or displace an earlier procedure that permitted such dismissals, without hearing or appeal, on national security grounds. The Court treated the issue solely as one of statutory construction and not as a due process issue.

Less clear are the procedural rights of those high level, policymaking employees who may still be hired and fired on the basis of political party affiliation, as we saw in chapter IV. While such persons would not likely be found to have a "property" interest in continuing employment if their party lost power, a "liberty" claim could possibly be advanced in a rare case. For the most part, though, such persons simply take public jobs with fewer guarantees and protections than their lower-level, less visible co-workers enjoy.

### If an internal procedure is provided by law, must an employee follow that procedure before going to court?

In general, yes. Courts usually require that those who seek review of agency actions have pursued any internal process that is available—that they have "exhausted their remedies." This policy reflects valid interests. The dispute may be no more than a minor misunderstanding that could easily be resolved, for example through an informal conference. Even where that is not possible, an internal process may narrow and sharpen the issues and develop a record that might be useful to a reviewing court. The time and cost of going outside the agency are obviously far greater for both sides. Thus there are many practical factors that support the concept of exhaustion of internal remedies.

There is at least one possible exception to the exhaustion requirement. If the internal review process is clearly not responsive or adequate to the employee's needs and would not have brought any meaningful relief, or if pursuing the internal channels would have forfeited external relief, then the employee may be permitted to go directly outside. But such a course is risky; a court may well conclude that the internal channels should have been followed and will send the matter back to the agency after time and money have been wasted in going initially outside.

There is one other related issue—the public worker's "election" of, or choice among, available remedies. When an employee seeks redress from the agency or through other state administrative channels and later sues in federal court on constitutional grounds, it may be argued that the initial state appeal was an "election" that foreclosed other remedies. A 1992 federal decision involving a group of Oregon state workers helps to clarify the situation in a way that is favorable to employee interests. While an employee would be barred from litigating again in federal court the precise issues that a state court had already decided, simply seeking relief through state channels would not have that effect. Thus, the appeals court declared: "[W]hen an employee of a state or local government entity presents a claim for reinstatement to a state administrative agency, that is not an election of remedies that will preclude the later pursuit of claims for violation of federal constitutional rights in federal court."[84] The court left open situations in which federal action might be precluded on other grounds relating to choice of state-law remedies.

## Must an agency follow its own procedures if those procedures are more generous than the Constitution requires?

Yes. The Supreme Court has several times held that if an agency creates a procedure—a hearing right, for example—that procedure may not be avoided or dispensed even if it gives more process than is due under the Constitution.[85] The agency or legislature may repeal the entire procedure if it wishes but may not withdraw or limit that procedure in particular cases so long as it remains on the books. Thus an employee may sometimes receive more process than the constitutional guarantees simply because the agency or the legislature has chosen to be more generous.

### May the hearing requirements be satisfied by due process in some other forum?

Yes, if the alternative process is available "at a meaningful time and in a meaningful manner." Thus in the *Loudermill* case the Supreme Court found that Ohio's informal pretermination approach satisfied due process largely because of the more elaborate posttermination appeal a discharged employee could pursue.[86] The Court then left open such questions as how long the posttermination appeal might be deferred (nine months was not too long); and what must be the contents of the later hearing or review. That case and others do not fully resolve the question to what degree a due process right may be satisfied in a completely different forum, such as a general public employee appeals body like the federal government's Merit Systems Protection Board, which serves the entire federal civil service rather than assigning hearings to each federal agency.

### How does collective bargaining affect procedural rights of public employees?

When a public employee union and government have agreed on procedures for redress of employee grievances, those channels are usually exclusive of any alternative avenues of redress. Members of the union and the agency both would be bound to follow those procedures. Only in a rare case might an aggrieved employee show that the union and the agency together had bargained away a right—either of substance or procedure—that was protected by the Constitution. In such a case the Constitution is of course paramount, and any contrary provision of the agreement would presumably be struck or modified—just as courts have in fact done in cases involving use of required union dues for purposes that would abridge the constitutional rights of public workers who are compelled by law to pay those dues.

## NOTES

1. 15th Report of the United States Civil Service Commission, p. 70 (1897–98), Rule II.

2. 5 U.S.C. § 7501 *et seq.* (1988).

3. Pub. L. No. 95–454, 92 Stat. 1111 (1978) (codified in scattered sections of Titles 5, 10, 15, 28, 39, and 42 U.S.C (1988)).

4. *Bush v. Lucas*, 462 U.S. 367, 385 (1983).

5. Note, 27 *Willammette L. Rev.* 803, 826 (1991).

6. 5 U.S.C. §§ 7104–7105 (1988).

7. 5 U.S.C. § 1201 *et seq.* (1988).

8. 5 U.S.C. § 4302e (1988).

9. 5 U.S.C. §§ 4303, 7503, 7512 (1988).

10. *See* Washington Post, May 31, 1991, at B2, cols. 1–2.

11. 5 U.S.C. § 4303 (1988).

12. 5 U.S.C. § 7503 (1988).

13. 5 U.S.C. § 7512 (1988).

14. 5 U.S.C. § 7701 (1988).

15. 5 U.S.C. § 7703(c) (1988).

16. *California Department of Human Resources Development v. Java*, 402 U.S. 121 (1971); *Goldberg v. Kelly*, 397 U.S. 254 (1970).

17. *Dixon v. Alabama State Board of Education*, 294 F.2d 150 (5th Cir. 1961).

18. *Bell v. Burson*, 402 U.S. 535 (1971); Morrissey v. Brewer, 408 U.S. 471 (1972).

19. *Fuentes v. Shevin*, 407 U.S. 67 (1972); *Sniadach v. Family Finance Corp.*, 395 U.S. 337 (1969).

20. 408 U.S. 564 (1972).

21. 408 U.S. 593 (1972).

22. 408 U.S. at 597–98.

23. 408 U.S. at 577.

24. 408 U.S. at 602.

25. *Bhargave v. Cloer*, 355 F. Supp. 1143 (N.D. Ga. 1972).

26. 426 U.S. 341 (1976).

27. 426 U.S. at 354.

28. 470 U.S. 532 (1985).

29. Ohio Rev. Code Ann. § 124 (1984).

30. *Loudermill v. Cleveland Board of Education*, 721 F.2d 550 (6th Cir. 1983).

31. 470 U.S. at 542–43.

32. 470 U.S. at 543.

33. 470 U.S. at 544.

34. 470 U.S. at 541.

35. *Bettio v. Village of Northfield*, 775 F. Supp. 1545 (N.D. Ohio 1991).

36. *Brewer v. Parkman*, 918 F.2d 1336 (8th Cir. 1990).

37. *Johnson v. Fraley*, 470 F.2d 179 (4th Cir. 1972).

38. *Roth v. Board of Regents*, 408 U.S. 564, 573 (1972).

39. 408 U.S. at 575.
40. *Adams v. Walker*, 492 F.2d 1003 (7th Cir. 1974).
41. *Willner v. Minnesota State Junior College Board*, 487 F.2d 153 (8th Cir. 1973); *Churchwell v. United States*, 414 F. Supp. 499 (D.S.D. 1976).
42. Note, "Due Process Rights of Public Employees," 50 *N.Y.U.L. Rev.* 310, 333 (1975).
43. *Vukadinovich v. Board of School Trustees*, 776 F. Supp. 1325 (N.D. Ind. 1991).
44. *Codd v. Velger*, 429 U.S. 624, 628 (1977).
45. *Siegert v. Gilley*, 114 L. Ed. 2d 277, *reh'g denied*, 114 L. Ed. 2d 1084 (1991).
46. 114 L. Ed. 2d at 278.
47. 114 L. Ed. 2d at 293.
48. 426 U.S. 341 (1976).
49. 426 U.S. at 348–49.
50. *Buxton v. Plant City, Fla.*, 871 F.2d 1037 (11th Cir. 1989).
51. *Mt. Healthy City School District Board of Education v. Doyle*, 429 U.S. 274 (1977).
52. 429 U.S. at 287.
53. *Board of Regents v. Roth*, 408 U.S. at 574, n. 13.
54. 408 U.S. at 578.
55. *See Hostrop v. Board of Junior Colleges*, 471 F.2d 488 (7th Cir. 1972).
56. *Hortonville Joint School District No. 1 v. Hortonville Education Association*, 426 U.S. 482 (1976).
57. *Matthews v. Harney County School Dist. No. 4*, 819 F.2d 889, 893 (9th Cir. 1987).
58. *Staton v. Mayes*, 552 F.2d 908, 914 (10th Cir.), *cert. denied*, 434 U.S. 907 (1977).
59. *Buschi v. Kirven*, 775 F.2d 1240, 1243 (4th Cir. 1985).
60. *Duchesne v. Williams*, 849 F.2d 1004 (6th Cir. 1988) (en banc), *cert. denied*, 109 S. Ct. 1535 (1989).
61. 416 U.S. 134 (1974).
62. *Cleveland Board of Education v. Loudermill*, 470 U.S. 532 (1985).
63. 470 U.S. at 544.
64. 470 U.S. at 544.
65. 470 U.S. at 544.
66. 470 U.S. at 544–45.
67. 470 U.S. at 546.
68. 470 U.S. at 546.
69. 470 U.S. at 546.
70. 470 U.S. at 546.
71. 470 U.S. at 546.

72. 470 U.S. at 546.
73. 470 U.S. at 547.
74. 470 U.S. at 547.
75. 470 U.S. at 553–59.
76. *Battle v. Mulholland*, 439 F.2d 321 (5th Cir. 1971).
77. *Snead v. Civil Service Commission*, 355 F. Supp. 764 (S.D.N.Y. 1973), 389 F. Supp. 935 (S.D.N.Y.), *vacated and remanded*, 421 U.S. 982 (1975).
78. *Muscare v. Quinn*, 520 F.2d 1212 (7th Cir. 1975), *cert. dismissed*, 425 U.S. 560 (1976).
79. *Buggs v. City of Minneapolis*, 358 F. Supp. 1340 (D. Minn. 1973).
80. *Adock v. Board of Education*, 109 Cal. Rptr. 676, 513 P.2d 900 (1973).
81. *Bottcher v. Florida Department of Agriculture and Consumer Services*, 361 F. Supp. 1123 (N.D. Fla. 1973).
82. *Norlander v. Schleck*, 345 F. Supp. 595 (D. Minn. 1972).
83. *Carlucci v. Doe*, 488 U.S. 93 (1988).
84. *Haphey v. Linn County, Ore.*, 953 F.2d 549, 552 (9th Cir. 1992).
85. *E.g.*, *Vitarelli v. Seaton*, 359 U.S. 535 (1959).
86. *Cleveland Board of Education v. Loudermill*, 470 U.S. 532, 536 (1985).

# VIII

## The Legal System

For many persons, law appears to be magic—an obscure domain that can be fathomed only by the professional initiated into its mysteries. People who might use the law to their advantage sometimes avoid the effort out of awe for its intricacies. But in fact the main lines of the legal system, and of the law in a particular area, can be explained in terms clear to the layperson. The purpose of this short chapter is to outline some important elements of the system.

### What does a lawyer mean by saying that a person has a legal right?

Having a right means that society has given a person permission—through the legal system—to secure some action or to act in some way that she or he desires. For example, a woman might have a right to an abortion, a minority person the right to employment free from discrimination, or a person accused of a crime the right to an attorney.

### How does one enforce a legal right?

The concept of *enforcing* a right gives meaning to the concept of the right itself. While the abstract right may be significant because it carries some connotation of morality and justice, enforcing the right yields something concrete—the abortion, the job, the attorney.

A person enforces her or his right by going to some appropriate authority—often, a judge—who has the power to take certain action. The judge can order the people who are refusing to grant the right to start doing so, on pain of going to jail if they disobey. The judge can also order the people to pay money to compensate for the loss of the right. Sometimes other authorities, such as federal and state administrative agencies or a labor arbitrator, can take similar remedial action.

The problem with the enforcement process is that it will often be lengthy, time-consuming, expensive, frustrating, and may arouse hostility in others—in short, it may not be worth the effort. On the other hand, in some cases you may not need to go to an enforcement authority in order to implement your right. The concerned persons or officials may not have realized that you have a right and may voluntarily change their actions once you explain your position. Then, too, they may not want to go through the legal process either—it can be as expensive and frustrating for them as it is for you.

### Where are legal rights defined?

There are several sources. Rights are defined in the statutes or laws passed by the U.S. Congress and by state and city legislatures. They are also set forth in the written decisions of judges, federal and state. Congress and state and local legislatures have also created institutions called administrative agencies to enforce certain laws, and these agencies interpret the laws in written decisions and rules that further define people's rights.

### Are rights always clearly defined and evenly applied to all people?

Not at all, although this is one of the great myths about law. Because so many different sources define people's rights, and because persons of diverse backgrounds and beliefs implement and enforce the law, there is virtually no way to uniformity. Nor do statutes that set forth rights always do so with clarity or specificity. It remains for courts or administrative agencies to interpret and flesh out the details; and in the process of doing so, many of the interpreters differ. Sometimes two different courts will give completely different answers to the same question. Whether or not a person has a particular right may depend on which state or city he or she lives in.

The more times a particular issue is decided, the more guidance there is in predicting what other judges or administrative personnel will decide. Similarly, the importance of the court or agency deciding a case or the persuasiveness of its reasoning will help determine the effect of the decision. A judge who states thoughtful reasons for a decision will have more influence than one who offers poor reasons.

Law then is not a preordained set of doctrines, applied rigidly and unswervingly in every situation. Rather, law is molded from the arguments and decisions of many persons and institutions. It is very much a human process of trying to convince others—a judge, a jury, an administrator, the lawyer for the other side—that your view of what the law requires is correct.

### What is a decision or case?

Lawyers often use these words interchangeably, although technically they do not mean the same thing. A case means the lawsuit started by one person against another, and it can refer to that lawsuit at any time from the moment it is started until the final result is reached. A decision means the written opinion in which the judge declares who wins the lawsuit and why.

### What is meant by precedent?

Precedent means past decisions. Lawyers use precedent to influence new decisions. If the facts involved in the prior decision are close to the facts in the present case, a judge will be strongly tempted to follow the former decision. She is not, however, bound to do so and, if persuasive reasons are presented to show that the prior decision was wrong or ill-suited to changed conditions in society, the judge may not follow precedent.

### What is the relationship between decisions and statutes?

In our legal system, most legal concepts originally were defined in the decisions of judges. In deciding what legal doctrine to apply to any case, each judge kept building on what other judges had done before him. The body of legal doctrines created in this way is called the common law.

The common law still applies in many situations, but increasingly state legislatures and the Congress pass laws ("statutes") to define the legal concepts that judges or agencies should use in deciding cases. The written decisions of individual judges are still important even where there is a statute because statutes are generally not specific enough to cover every set of facts. Judges have to interpret the meaning of statutes, apply them to the facts at hand, and write a decision; that decision will then be considered by other judges when they deal with these statutes in other cases. Thus it is generally not enough to know what a relevant statute defines as illegal; you also have to know how judges have interpreted the statute in specific situations.

## What different kinds of courts are there?

The United States is unique for its variety of courts. Broadly speaking, there are two distinct court systems: federal and state. Both are located throughout the country; each is limited to certain kinds of cases, with substantial areas of overlap. Most crimes are prosecuted in state courts, for instance, although there a number of federal crimes prosecuted in federal court. People must always use state courts to get a divorce (except in the District of Columbia and other federal areas), but they must sue in federal court to establish rights under certain federal laws.

In both federal and state court systems one starts out at the trial court level, where the facts are "tried." This means that a judge or jury listens and watches as the lawyers present evidence of the facts that each side seeks to prove. Evidence can take many forms: written documents, the testimony of a witness on the stand, photographs, charts. Once a judge or jury has listened to or observed all the evidence presented by each side, it will choose the version of the facts it believes, apply the applicable legal doctrine to these facts, and decide which side has won. If either side is unhappy with the result, it may be able to take the case to the next, higher-level court and argue that the judge or the jury applied the wrong legal concept to the facts, or that no reasonable jury or judge could have found the facts as they were found in the trial court, and that the result was therefore wrong.

## What are plaintiffs and defendants?

The plaintiff is the person who sues—that is, who *complains* that someone has wronged him or her and asks the court to remedy this situation. The defendant is the person sued—or the one who *defends* herself against the charges of the plaintiff. The legal writing in which the plaintiff articulates her or his basic grievance is the *complaint*, and a lawsuit is generally commenced by filing this document with the clerk at the courthouse. The defendant then responds to these charges in a document appropriately named an *answer*. Some states use different names for these documents.

One refers to a particular lawsuit by giving the names of the plaintiff and defendant. If Mary Jones sues Smith Corporation for refusing to hire her because she is a woman, her case will be called *Jones v. Smith Corporation* (v. stands for versus or against).

### What is an administrative agency?

Agencies are institutions established by either state or federal legislatures to administer or enforce a particular law or series of laws and are distinct from both courts and legislature. They often regulate a particular industry. For example, the Federal Communications Commission regulates the broadcasting industry (radio and television stations and networks) and the telephone and telegraph industry, in accordance with the legal standards set forth in the Federal Communications Act; and the Interstate Commerce Commission regulates trucking and railroads.

These agencies establish legal principles, referred to as rules, regulations, or guidelines. Rules are interpretations of a statute and are designed to function in the same way as a statute—to define people's rights and obligations on a general scale, but in a more detailed fashion than the statute itself. Agencies also issue specific decisions in particular cases, like a judge, applying a law or rule to a factual dispute between particular parties.

### How does one find court decisions, statutes, and agency rules and decisions?

All these materials are published and can be found in law libraries. In order to find the item desired, one should understand the system lawyers use for referring to, or citing, these materials. Some examples will help clarify the system. A case might be cited as *Watson v. Limbach Company*, 333 F. Supp. 754 (S.D. Ohio 1971); a statute, as 42 U.S.C. § 1983; a regulation, as 29 C.F.R. § 1604.10(b). The unifying factor in all three citations is that the first number denotes the particular volume in a series of books with the same title; the words or the letters that follow represent the name of the book; and the second number represents either the page or the section in the identified volume. In the examples above, the *Watson* case is found in the 333rd volume of the series of books called *Federal Supplement* at page 754; the statute is found in volume 42 of the series called the *United States Code* at Section 1983; the regulation is in volume 29 of the *Code of Federal Regulations* at Section 1604.10(b).

There are similar systems for state court decisions. Once you understand the system, all you need do is find out from the librarian where any particular series of books is kept, then look up the proper volume and page or section. It is also important to look for the same page or section in the material sometimes inserted at the back of a book, since many legal materials are periodically updated. A librarian will tell you what any abbreviations stand for if you are unfamiliar with that series.

Given this basic information, anyone can locate and read important cases, statutes, and regulations. Throughout the book, such materials have been cited when deemed particularly important, and laypersons are urged to read them. Although lawyers often use overly technical language, the references cited in this book can be comprehended without serious difficulty, and reading the original legal materials will give public employees a deeper understanding of their rights.

### What is the role of the lawyer in the legal system?

A lawyer understands the intricacies and technicalities of the legal system, can maneuver within it efficiently, and, is able to help other people by doing so. Thus the lawyer knows where to find out about the leading legal doctrines in any given area and how to predict the outcome of your case, based on a knowledge of those doctrines. A lawyer can advise you what to do: forget about the case; take it to an administrative agency; sue in court; make a will; and so on. The lawyer then can help you take the legal actions that you determine are necessary.

### How are legal costs determined and how do they affect people's rights?

The cost of using the legal system is predominantly the cost of paying the lawyer for his or her time. Since this has become prohibitive even for middle-class individuals, many people are not able to assert their rights, even though they might ultimately win if they had the money to pay a lawyer for doing the job.

### Is legal action the only way to win one's legal rights?

By no means. Negotiation, education, consciousness raising, publicity, demonstrations, organization, and lobbying are all ways to achieve rights, often more effectively that through the standard but costly and time-consuming resort to the courts. In all these areas, it helps to have secure knowledge of the legal underpinning of your rights. One has a great deal more authority if one is protesting illegal action. The refrain "That's illegal" may move some people in and of itself; or it may convince those with whom you are dealing that you're serious enough to do something about the situation—by starting a lawsuit, for instance.